Christian youth are facing more
in history. Unfortunately, many Christian parents are not equipped to mentor their own children. Reasons for Hope is an excellent ministry, and their book, Did Jesus Commit Suicide? is an exceptional resource for every Christian.

—Jay Seegert

Author of Creation & Evolution: Compatible or In Conflict?

Founder and Director of The Starting Point Project

As Christian parents, ministers, and influencers of the next generation, we need to be ready with gracious and reasonable answers. If you are looking for a resource that will help you better understand and reach the next generation for Jesus Christ, I cannot recommend this book highly enough!

—Jason Carlson

President of Christian Ministries International

Bold teens asking bold questions and getting bold answers. That pretty well sums up Carl Kerby's newest book, Did Jesus Commit Suicide—and 27 Other Questions Teens Are Asking. Written in a down-to-earth, straight-forward, conversational style, this book is very much needed for teens—and for parents and youth leaders—if we are going to have a generation that will truly 'Stay bold' for the Savior and His truth.

—Julaine Appling

President of Wisconsin Family Action

Teens today are faced with a growing number of perplexing questions that challenge their faith. Abandoning any hope that there are solid answers, their faith erodes, their foundation crumbles and sadly, many are joining the ranks of skeptics and scoffers. Addressing this critical matter, (the) writers tackle these questions head-on by upholding the absolute authority of God's Word to present solid Biblical answers to these questions. The reader is left encouraged, strengthened, and firmly established in biblical truth.

—Jim Schneider

Executive Director of VCY America

Host of CrossTalk America and InFocus-TV

Did Jesus Commit Suicide?

and

27 Other Questions
Teens Are Asking About the Bible
(that adults want to know, too)

Edited by **Carl Kerby** and **Juan Valdes**

reasons*for***hope***

Did Jesus Commit Suicide?
And 27 Other Questions Teens Are Asking About the Bible
(that adults want to know, too)

Published by:
Reasons for Hope
208 Sherman Street
Jackson, MN 56143

For more information, call or write:
1-800-552-HOPE (4673)
info@rforh.com

ISBN: 978-1-938966-17-0
Third Printing

Written and compiled by friends and employees of Reasons for Hope.
(See "About the Authors/Editors" section at the end of this book for more detail.)
Edited by Carl Kerby and Juan Valdes
Editors/Proofreaders: Hannah Dukes and Holly Varnum
Cover Design and Interior Layout by Ben Cole
Creative Direction by Bub Kuns
Illustrations by Dan Lietha

Printed in the United States of America

ACKNOWLEDGEMENTS

CARL KERBY

This book is fulfilling a ministry dream that goes back to January 8, 2011, when Reasons for Hope first started. From the beginning, our heart has been to reach a younger generation and encourage adults in their faith. When we initiated this project, we really had no idea where it would go—we just knew we had to do it. Let me begin by thanking key supporters who pushed us to go after the issues addressed within these pages.

When you read studies about why the younger generation doesn't trust the Word of God and why so many end up walking away from their faith, the statistics always involve questions that were never answered or *inadequate* answers to their questions. This being the case, we took the approach that we did: We asked teens what issues were posing the biggest questions or doubts about their faith, and we addressed them deeply enough to provide the substance needed, but "lightly" enough to keep their attention.

I have to give a huge shout out to Hannah Dukes, Holly Varnum, Juan Valdes, Bub Kuns, and Ben Cole. These folks did the heavy lifting for this project and pulled it off. I'd also like to thank our printer, The Copy Center Plus, as they have been so gracious to us and pulled out all the stops to make the printing of this book happen quickly.

Lastly, and most importantly we must thank the Lord Jesus Christ for putting this eclectic team together and giving us the desire to pursue things that aren't so comfortable sometimes. Some of these questions are tough, and there really isn't an easy answer to them. We've done our best and will leave the rest up to the Holy Spirit. Please, come quickly, Lord Jesus!

CONTENTS

PART FOUR: BIBLICAL ANSWERS

PART FIVE: THE CHARACTER OF GOD

WELCOME TO THE BATTLE!

We may not like to admit it, but, yes, we are in a spiritual battle, and it can feel overwhelming! Since oftentimes in this battle, it's the younger generation that is facing the heaviest attack, we decided that we were going to place a special emphasis on reaching youth and equipping parents. At Reasons for Hope, our marching orders are: "To train and equip the next generation to stand boldly on the Word of God!"

This book is one of the ways we can accomplish that. It is a compilation of the most-asked questions given to all of our speakers combined, and each one of these questions actually came from a teen or a youth in their 20's. One vitally important lesson we have learned is that instead of us telling youth what the issues are, we have to let them tell us!

To find out what's really running through their minds on day one of a camp week, we hand out index cards to the attendees and tell them: *"Write down the questions that are keeping you from selling out for the Lord Jesus Christ, because THAT'S what we'll be addressing while we're with you."*

Trust me when I tell you that IT WORKS! The first time I did this, the camp directors were VERY skeptical. They had scheduled me to speak once in the morning and once in the evening every day. I asked them for additional speaking times, and they told me that it just wouldn't work, because they had "free time" in the afternoon so the kids could enjoy the ziplining, boating, disc golfing, etc.–all the "fun" stuff!

I told them that we could make it a voluntary session and whoever came, came! I didn't care if only one student showed up, I'd give that one everything I had. If no one showed up, so be it! Well, guess what? Over two-thirds of the youth came to the voluntary session at that camp!

Every time that I've done this since, the results have been the same. YOUTH CARE! Don't let anyone deceive you into thinking that the younger generation isn't interested in spiritual things. They're VERY interested, but you better bring your "A" game if you want to reach them.

The bottom line is, today's youth think differently than they used to, even ten years ago. They want something that is real, direct, honest, and relevant to the world they live in. I recently read a perfect example of why youth are walking away from Christianity in a secular book entitled, *iGen: Why Today's Super–Connected Kids Are Growing Up Less Rebellious, More Tolerant, Less Happy–and Completely Unprepared for Adulthood and What That Means for the Rest of Us.* I know, long title, but amazing information if you want to reach today's youth. Jean Twinge, the author, on page 139 in her book, states that, "...many young people feel a disconnect between their church and what they experience outside of it, including science, pop culture, and sexuality. For example, half of 13- to 17-year-olds want to pursue a science-related career. Yet only 1% of youth pastors say they have addressed any subject related to science in the last year." There's MUCH MORE evidence that backs this up as well.

The questions we've included in this book reveal some of the issues that youth are struggling with, and to reach this generation, we must be able to show how the Bible directly addresses these issues. Teaching critical thinking and a biblical worldview to this younger generation needs to become our number one priority after the preaching of the Gospel!

Reasons for Hope has been blessed over the years to compile an amazing team of teachers/speakers, and this has been a team project for us. We even brought in some outside experts to get the best responses possible. The book of Proverbs tells us there is wisdom in godly counsel, and I greatly appreciate each and every one of the folks who have made this book a reality. As a young Christian, I would have loved to have a book like this addressing the issues I was struggling with. Thus, I'm very happy that we can now put this in the hands of the youth, parents, teachers, pastors, and anyone who loves and cares about the young people in their lives.

Note to parents: YOU CAN DO THIS! You need to study these things and have answers for your children. Our desire is that these resources will make you the hero to your children. Please make sure to download our app: just go to your App Store and search for "Reasons for Hope." Look for the blue asterisk "*" after the title. There are MANY more resources there for you to use FREE OF CHARGE! May God richly bless and keep you. Let us know how we can serve you and most importantly, Stay Bold!

Writers/Editors
Carl Kerby
Juan Valdes

Editors/Proofreaders
Hannah Dukes
Holly Varnum

Contributing writers:
Hannah Dukes
Frank Figueroa
Dave Glander
Marc Jacobs
Bub Kuns
Dan Lietha
Candace Nordine
Dr. David Ross
Brian Scoggin

Illustrator
Dan Lietha

PART ONE

SOCIAL/CULTURAL CONCERNS

Chapter 1

DID JESUS COMMIT SUICIDE? ISN'T THAT A SIN?

Original question: If suicide is a sin, didn't Jesus commit suicide on the cross?[1]

JUAN VALDES

Since the Bible clearly teaches that Jesus voluntarily chose to die, the obvious question arises, did Jesus commit the sin of suicide or not? While natural death can be the result of an accident, an illness, a crime, or old age, suicide is different. A person who dies in an accident does not choose to die; death surprises them. A person who passes away from an illness or old age usually does not desire death. Those that die

[1]Imagine, you're sitting in front of over 500 youth that you've encouraged to write down and submit any question that's keeping them from completely trusting Jesus Christ. MANY have taken you up on the offer and you have an approximately two-inch tall stack of index cards containing the questions they've written down sitting in front of you. You DON'T work your way through them, picking and choosing which you feel the most comfortable addressing; you just have to take each one as it comes up next in the stack. Things have gone well for about twenty minutes, and then you pull out the following question. (Yes, this happened to me!) CK

as a result of a crime did *not* choose to die that day. Unlike the other forms of death, where the person did not choose to die, suicide is a deliberate choice to end one's life.

How one responds to the question above, therefore, has the potential to unearth serious theological inconsistencies. If Jesus' death is considered a suicide, it can no longer be said that Jesus was sinless … and it's all downhill from there. Therefore, this question merits *serious* consideration. The short answer to the question is that the death of Jesus on the cross was **not** death by suicide, thus Jesus did not sin, but that response needs to be clarified.

WHAT IS THE SIN OF SUICIDE?

Clearly defining our terms is of utmost importance if one is to judge whether the death of Jesus qualifies as suicide or not. Although it seems obvious that suicide means killing oneself on purpose, it is important to consider a more formal definition. The CDC defines suicide as "death caused by injuring oneself with the intent to die."[2] It is also important to note that most of the time, people who commit suicide do so because they are under tremendous stress.[3] There is a connection between desiring to end one's own life and feelings of desperation, depression, hopelessness, etc. Are these feelings sinful?

While the emotions that lead to suicide are not necessarily sinful, the Bible makes it clear that taking one's own life is a grave sin. The sixth commandment states, "You shall not murder" (Exodus 20:13, NKJV). It seems rather obvious that it implies not murdering ourselves either. Paul makes the connection even clearer when he relates this and the other mandates with Jesus' teachings, concluding that they are "…all summed up in this saying…, 'You shall love your neighbor as yourself'" (Romans 13:9, NKJV). The assumption is that one does not engage in harmful behavior against oneself and consequently should treat their neighbor likewise. The gravity of the sin of suicide is because man is an image bearer of God, thus murder (including self-murder) is

---

[2]"Suicide Prevention: Facts About Suicide," *Centers for Disease Control and Prevention.* Accessed December 10, 2021. https://www.ede.gov/suicide/facts/index.html

[3]Nancy Schimelpfening, "Why Do People Commit Suicide?" *Verywell Mind.* Accessed December 10, 2021. https://www.verywellmind.com/why-do-people-commit-suicide-1067515

the taking of a life made in the image of God (Genesis 9:5-6). So, did Jesus commit the grave sin of suicide?

WAS HIS DEATH ON THE CROSS A SUICIDE?

No. Jesus did not "injure himself with the intent to die" as defined above. This is clear for at least three reasons.

- First, the injuries He suffered were not self-inflicted. The Romans were the ones who beat and crucified Him.
- Second, Jesus did not desire to die; a fact made obvious by His request, "O My Father, if it is possible, let this cup pass from Me; nevertheless, not as I will, but as You will" (Matthew 26:39, NKJV).
- Third, Jesus was not depressed and hopeless, but quite the contrary. Humanity was hopeless and Jesus was giving us a reason for hope.

The question then arises, didn't Jesus say that He laid down His own life and that no one took it from Him?

The passage in question is from John 10 where He states that "I lay down My life that I may take it again. No one takes it from Me, but I lay it down of Myself…" (John 10:17-18, NKJV). It is important to remember that verses must always be taken *in context*. Always. This entire chapter has Jesus referring to Himself as a shepherd. He speaks of Himself as the *true* shepherd in the first paragraph and then as the *good* shepherd in the immediate context of the verses in question. Most importantly, He is making a contrast between "the good shepherd" (Himself) and "the hireling." Notice the contrast.

> I am the good shepherd. *The good shepherd gives His life for the sheep.* But a hireling, he who is not the shepherd, one who does not own the sheep, sees the wolf coming and leaves the sheep and flees; and the wolf catches the sheep and scatters them. The hireling flees because he is a hireling and does not care about the sheep (John 10:11-13, NKJV, emphasis added).

What Jesus is emphasizing in verse 11 and again in verse 15 is that "*I lay down My life for the sheep.*" His death was not a suicide but a sacrifice. Jesus' death was analogous to that of a soldier in combat who heroically gives his life to save the lives of other soldiers. Christ demonstrated the greatest love of all by being willing to die to save the lives of His sheep. Just a few chapters later, He says, "Greater love has no one than this, than to lay down one's life for his friends" (John 15:13, NKJV). And yet, an even more important question arises from this one.

WHY DID JESUS HAVE TO DIE IN THE FIRST PLACE?

Jesus did not *have to* die. The Bible is clear that Jesus voluntarily *chose* to die. Jesus could have chosen not to die, in which case humanity would be lost in sin and separated from God forever. Jesus chose to die because we had accrued a debt to God that we were unable to pay. God's perfect justice demands that all transgressions receive just punishment. The punishment for man's transgression—his sinful aggression against God—is death. Jesus chose to die on our behalf because He loves us and does not want anyone to have to pay the ultimate price of death for their sins (Romans 3:23; 6:23). By choosing to die on our behalf, Jesus chose to pay the debt for our transgressions in full (Colossians 2:14, NKJV). But some may ask, "Couldn't God have saved man without Jesus having to die such a horrible death?"

Jesus' death was analogous to that of a soldier in combat who heroically gives his life to save the lives of other soldiers.

COULDN'T IT HAVE BEEN DONE ANOTHER WAY?

It is foolish, from our limited perspective, to question the wisdom of God's plan for redemption. Furthermore, it seems rather arrogant for man to believe he can come up with a "better plan" or a "better alternative" to God's plan. In His omniscience (the state or quality of knowing all things), God will always choose the best possible course of action in any given circumstance to accomplish His perfect will. Had there been a better way–a way that would have kept Christ off the cross–we can be sure God would have chosen it.

A quick survey of the two most common alternatives that have been proposed highlights the sharp contrast between man's foolishness and God's wisdom.

1. Some have argued that God could have created man without the option to sin, rendering Jesus' death unnecessary. While this sounds good, careful consideration reveals the folly. God created man perfect. Part of what makes us perfect is that God created us as free beings; we are not robots. Had God created us without freedom, that would not have been good; it would have been evil. While our freedom makes sin possible, it doesn't make it necessary. We choose to exploit our freedom when we sin. Nevertheless, God's plan accounted for our abuse of freedom and included a plan for redeeming man from his fallen state.
2. Others propose that God could have chosen to forgive everyone. This way Jesus didn't have to die on the cross, and everyone would go to Heaven. Once again, that sounds great, but upon closer consideration, it doesn't work either.
    - First, when man freely chooses to disobey God and is unrepentant, forgiveness and restoration is not possible (2 Corinthians 7:9,10).
    - Second, the idea seems to suggest that God is unwilling to forgive some people. This is not true! God's salvation and forgiveness are available to ALL who repent and believe (John 3:16-17, NKJV), but no one is forced to believe or accept it.
    - Furthermore, everyone going to Heaven would be a violation of man's free will—for there are many who do not want to go to Heaven. For those who freely choose to reject God, and who affirm that they want nothing to do with Him, being forced to spend an eternity with Him would be worse than Hell.

   C.S. Lewis said it well in his book, *The Great Divorce*: "There are only two kinds of people in the end: those who say to God, 'Thy will be done,' and those to whom God says, in the end, 'Thy will be done.'"

CONCLUSION

In His wisdom, God devised a plan by which HE pays the debt demanded by His justice and makes righteousness available through Jesus Christ to all who believe.

One of the things that sets Christianity apart from all other religions is God's perfect justice juxtaposed with God's perfect mercy! God's justice is perfect: every transgression—no matter how small—must be paid for. God does not turn a blind eye on any sin—regardless of who commits it. That is perfect justice! However, God's mercy is also perfect! God loves all of humanity with perfect love and does not desire that anyone should perish. In His wisdom, God devised a plan by which HE pays the debt demanded by His justice and makes righteousness available through Jesus Christ to all who believe. That is perfect mercy! That is why Jesus chose not to commit suicide, but to die a *sacrificial* death; it could not have been done any other way. There is no greater plan for redemption!

Chapter 2

WHY DOES GOD CREATE HOMOSEXUALS AND THEN CONDEMN THEM?

JUAN VALDES

We are all broken. We all struggle with sin. The ONLY difference between a Christian and a non-Christian is our saving relationship with Jesus. We have found the Way, the Truth, and the Life—Jesus (John 14:6). We have found forgiveness for our brokenness. We have found a source of strength that enables us to overcome our weaknesses on a daily basis. We have found the only way to be at peace with God—Jesus. We have found the only way to enter eternity with God—Jesus.

Thus, the only way to properly address this question is from a level playing field—we have all sinned and have fallen short of the glory of God. However, this question specifically addressed the sin of homosexuality, so let's break it down into three distinct but interconnected questions to cover this issue. First, did God create us as broken individuals? Second, are people born homosexual? Third, are we condemned by our inclinations?

DID GOD CREATE US AS BROKEN INDIVIDUALS?

The short answer is NO, but let's unpack that a little. Humankind today does not reflect God's original design. When God created humans, He created them as morally perfect individuals that reflected His image. Prior to the first sin, Adam and Eve did not struggle with brokenness. Because their free will had not yet been tested, they had not participated in any type of behavior or attitude that displeased God. They were perfect, and that was God's intention for mankind. God did not create homosexuals, just like He did not create thieves, liars, alcoholics, drug addicts, adulterers, slanderers, etc. So, what happened?

Why do we all struggle with brokenness? Why is it that we are born with a tendency to sin? The answer is found in Genesis 3—the fall. Part of mankind's perfection was his freedom. God created Adam and Eve with a will and the freedom to exercise it. In order to exercise their free will, God provided Adam and Eve a choice to obey or disobey Him. We all know the rest of the story—Adam and Eve exercised their free will and chose to disobey God. In doing so, brokenness (sin) was introduced into humanity. But why does that apply to everyone else? Why is it that everyone is born with an inclination towards sin?

Why is it that everyone is born with an inclination towards sin?

There are various approaches to this question, but let's keep it simple. First, let's consider an analogy. If a perfect seed is contaminated with imperfection, then planted in the ground, the resulting tree will carry that imperfection. And every other tree that comes from the seeds of that tree will continue to carry the imperfection. Because Adam and Eve were contaminated, their offspring, along with all future generations, would carry the imperfection.

Another way of approaching this question is through the lens of genetics. Adam and Eve's genome was perfect. In other words, their DNA was perfect. Perfect DNA can only reproduce perfectly. However, their act of disobedience introduced imperfection into their bodies. When God warned them not to eat of the forbidden fruit or they would die, He was not speaking only of spiritual death (separation from God) but also physical death. Their perfect genome would no longer be perfect—they were broken now, and physical death would be inevitable. Further, the imperfection in the DNA would only get worse with every passing generation. That is exactly what we observe in the world of genetics. Every successive generation has several more significant mutations than the previous generation. That explains, for instance, why we see birth defects and why babies are born with leukemia or Down syndrome. So, does this also affect our sense of morality?

If our genome is deteriorating, so are all our natural functions and abilities. For example, a perfect mind makes perfect decisions, every time, but a corrupted mind is more likely to make corrupted decisions. The more corrupt our genome becomes, the more likely we are to make bad decisions. Hence, there is a connection between our brokenness and our choices. Furthermore, there is strong conclusive evidence in genetics that certain behaviors or tendencies in parents can be passed down to future generations. For example, it is common knowledge that around 50% of a person's susceptibility to drug or alcohol addiction can be traced to genetics.[4] We know that addictions affect the brain—there is a rewiring of brain circuits directly related to rewards and gratifications. This rewiring is strengthened through repetition. It is believed that this rewiring somehow affects our genome—which may explain why it is often transferred to the next generation. There is much that remains a mystery in the field of genetics and heredity, but we know enough to see that imperfections (mutations) are often transferred genetically to future generations. However, it is important to clarify that having the inclination doesn't determine the behavior—there is still a choice factor. The Bible clearly teaches that though we are born with the inclination to sin (Psalm 51:5; 58:3), we still must make the conscious choice to act on our inclinations.

However, it is important to clarify that having the inclination doesn't control the behavior—there is still a choice factor.

[4]Tatiana Foroud, et al, "Genetic research: Who is at risk for alcoholism?" *Alcohol research & health: the journal of the National Institute on Alcohol Abuse and Alcoholism,* vol. 33, 1-2 (2010): 64-75.

ARE PEOPLE BORN HOMOSEXUAL?

Short answer: NO and YES. If the question is whether there is a "gay gene" that somehow predetermines homosexuality, the answer, so far, is NO. Just like there is no "adultery gene" or "lying gene" or any general "sin gene," geneticists have never found a "gay gene." Nevertheless, even if such a gene is found, that doesn't justify the behavior any more than a "murder gene" would justify murder or a "stealing gene" would justify stealing. It would only serve to identify where the brokenness happens in the genome. But there is no reason to believe that a person is born gay.

On the other hand, if the question is whether some people are born with an inclination to same-sex attraction, the answer is YES. Think about it. We don't usually choose who we are attracted to. Some men are attracted to dark-skinned brunettes while others are attracted to light-skinned blondes. Women, too, are often attracted to specific types of men. Often, there are people we find attractive and others that we don't—and there doesn't seem to be any rhyme nor reason for it. Similarly, some men are naturally attracted to other men, and some women are naturally attracted to other women, and it appears to be hardwired. In addition, many people who struggle with same-sex attraction do not want it—they reject it. We cannot say that they choose to have these attractions, because they don't. I have counseled many broken-hearted young people who pray that God would take away their same-sex attractions, because they don't want them. My heart aches for them. Is it a sin to be inclined that way? NO. We all have inclinations towards sin. Furthermore, we must clarify that our desires don't define us. Thank God for that, or I would often be defined as a murderer—especially when someone cuts me off in traffic. For a moment, it is my desire to grab that driver and … well, let's leave it at that. We are not defined by our desires; we are defined by our behavior–our choices. This leads us to the final question.

ARE WE CONDEMNED BY OUR INCLINATIONS?

We are condemned by our choices, not by our inclinations. Our choices, whether good or bad, have consequences. The Bible is clear that the consequence of sin is death (Romans 6:23). Since we have all sinned, we are all condemned. Homosexuality is not the only sin that is condemned; all sin is condemned. When man chooses to deliberately disobey God, he must deal with the resulting judgment. Is this unfair?

People often ask how God can judge and condemn them for something they cannot control? The problem with this question is that we absolutely CAN control our behavior. Man has never lost his free will. There is a big difference between having same-sex attractions and choosing to act on them, much like there is a big difference between desiring to steal something and choosing to steal it. Every sin begins as a desire (James 1:14). It's what we choose to do with that desire that makes all the difference (James 1:15). But is it realistic to expect someone to live a life of celibacy in order not to sin against God? Yes.

There are many men and women that struggle daily with same-sex attractions but choose to deny themselves. We all have similar battles. The addict must choose daily not to act on his desires. Those inclined towards adultery must choose daily not to act on their desires. Is it difficult for them? Of course, it is. Is it worth it? Absolutely. But what about those that have already sinned?

CONCLUSION

Welcome to the club of sinners—where nobody is denied admission. God knows that we have all sinned and that we all struggle with desires that don't please Him. God knows that we are all broken and weak, and that we sometimes fall.

The Apostle Paul expressed the amazing sense of relief he felt in knowing that his struggles with sin would not keep him from eternal life—because he was "in Jesus." After opening up about his own struggles with sin and expressing the frustration of wanting to be rid of the sinful desires (Romans 6-7), he begins the eighth chapter of Romans with this announcement, "There is therefore now no condemnation for those who are in Christ Jesus" (Romans 8:1).

This is where the good news comes into the picture. God has provided a way for us to escape condemnation—despite our sinful nature. We don't have to pay the ultimate price for our sins (eternal death) because Jesus' death on the cross paid for all of them. All we must do is trust Jesus for our salvation and surrender to His Lordship in our lives. Listen to these wonderful words of hope.

John 3:16-18; 1 Corinthians 15:56,57

For God so loved the world, that he gave his only Son, that whoever believes in him should not perish but have eternal life. For God did not send his Son into the world to condemn the world, but in order that the world might be saved through him. Whoever believes in him is not condemned, but whoever does not believe is condemned already, because he has not believed in the name of the only Son of God … The sting of death is sin, and the strength of sin is the law. But thanks be to God, who gives us the victory through our Lord Jesus Christ.

Chapter 3

WHY IS PORNOGRAPHY SO WRONG?

Bub Kuns

Believe it or not, this is a very popular question among teens and young adults ... and not just boys. Girls ask the question too; in fact, females make up over 30% of pornography watchers. Some people just throw this question out there as a smokescreen and don't really want to know the answer, but others really want to know what the big deal is about porn. After all, they aren't physically having sex with another person; they are just "watching."

To answer this question with grace and truth, we first need to understand why God created sex in the first place and then why He placed certain boundaries around it. Remember that it is God who has the sole privilege of defining what's bad (or *sinful*) and what's good (or *righteous*). The One who created sex and sexuality also has the right to set the boundaries for it.

MAN AND WOMAN

We find at the very beginning of the Bible, in Genesis 1:27, that it is written, "So God created man in His own image, in the image of God

He created him; **male** and **female** He created **them"** (emphasis added). In the very next verse, Genesis 1:28, it is written, "And God **blessed** them. And God said to them, "Be **fruitful and multiply** and fill the earth and subdue it and have dominion over the fish of the sea and over the birds of the heavens and over every living thing that moves on the earth" (emphasis added).

Here's a quick way to remember God's intentions for sex from the Genesis account: One man. One woman. One flesh. One lifetime. That's God's design.

Later, in Genesis 2:24, God says, "Therefore a **man** shall leave his father and his mother and **hold fast to his wife**, and they shall become **one flesh**" (emphasis added). He later pronounces this "very good." The Gospel of Matthew further illuminates this union by saying, "So they are no longer two but one flesh. What therefore God has joined together, let not man separate" (Matthew 19:6).

God is the One who introduced sex and sexuality and set boundaries for its expression. This means that sex is a sacred gift and meant to bring great joy and pleasure within the boundaries God has prescribed. Here are the boundaries we understand from the words in Genesis 1 and 2.

1. God created two genders (male and female). They are different but equal; they are dissimilar but complementary.
2. God directed the man and woman, and only man and woman (not man with man or woman with woman) to "be fruitful and multiply." Both the male and female are essential to create offspring; it's the only way to "multiply."
3. God bonds the man and woman as husband and wife (male and female) in marriage, and they should remain together for life.

Here's a quick way to remember God's intentions for sex from the Genesis account: One man. One woman. One flesh. One lifetime. That's God's design.

THE BIGGER CATEGORY

You might read that and say, "I'm not convinced just by the Genesis description." Well then, enter the Ten Commandments (first stated in Exodus 20). Both the seventh and tenth commandments apply to our topic here. The seventh commandment is this: "You shall not commit adultery." The tenth commandment is this: "You shall not covet your neighbor's house, you shall not covet your neighbor's wife, or his male servant, or his female servant, or his ox, or his donkey, or anything that is your neighbor's."

You may be saying, "What in the world do these verses have to do with pornography?" To answer that, we will first go to the words of Jesus and then the Apostle Paul. As we wrap up the discussion together, hopefully it will all make sense. Here are the words of Jesus in Matthew 5:27-30 (emphasis added):

> You have heard that it was said, "You shall not commit adultery." But I say to you that everyone **who looks at a woman with lustful intent** has already committed adultery with her in his heart. If your right eye causes you to sin, tear it out and throw it away. For it is better that you lose one of your members than that your whole body be thrown into hell. And if your right hand causes you to sin, cut it off and throw it away. For it is better that you lose one of your members than that your whole body go into hell

Ouch! I think that covers the pornography topic very clearly. If a man lusts after a woman, it is sin (and the same goes for a man lusting after another man or a woman lusting after a man or woman). If someone even "looks" at a woman (or man) with lustful intent, it is wrong. Pornography is ALL about lust. In God's eyes, lust is equal to adultery. It's a sin, period. There's no way around it. So sacred is the nature and act of sex to God that Jesus (using hyperbole to make sure we understand the seriousness of this issue) says it's better to lose an eye or a hand if those parts of your body lead you into sin.

THE DANGER OF SEXUAL IMMORALITY

Now let's read the words of the Apostle Paul:

1 Corinthians 6:9,18; Galatians 5:19-20
(***Bold*** *print indicates emphasis added.*)

> Or do you not know that the unrighteous will not inherit the kingdom of God? Do not be deceived: neither the **sexually immoral** [fornicators], nor idolaters, nor adulterers, nor men who practice homosexuality... Flee from **sexual immorality** [fornication]. Every other sin a person commits is outside the body, but the sexually immoral person sins against his own body … Now the works of the flesh are evident: **sexual immorality** [fornication], impurity, sensuality, idolatry, sorcery, enmity, strife, jealousy, fits of anger, rivalries, dissensions, divisions.

I emphasized "sexual immorality" and put a form of the word "to fornicate" here because that's the overarching category that includes ALL SEXUAL THOUGHTS AND ACTIVITIES outside the confines of marriage. Sexual immorality includes masturbation, viewing pornography, giving into sexual fantasies and thoughts, and a host of other things we don't have time to mention. In fact, the word "fornicate" is from the Greek word "porneia," from which we get the term pornography. That should tell you something!

CONNECTING THE DOTS

Now that we've seen the pattern and intent for sexual relationships in Genesis and read the words of Jesus and the Apostle Paul, let's get back to those two commandments mentioned earlier: "You shall not commit adultery" and "You shall not covet."

It's very simple: The Bible is absolutely clear that all sex outside of marriage is a form of adultery, and adultery is sin. If we look at another person on a screen, across a room, or through a window with lustful thoughts and desires, we are also coveting another person's daughter/son, wife/husband, girlfriend/boyfriend, etc. If we give into these temptations by entertaining these thoughts, we have broken at least two commandments. I would offer that we also are breaking the second commandment which is about idolatry, because you are worshipping sex and putting your desires above God's. Watching pornography is not only committing adultery, coveting, and idolatry, but it usually includes some form of deception, because often you are lying about it to family or friends. Clearly, it's bad all around.

The bottom line is that God has a beautiful plan and purpose for sex within the safe and loving boundaries of marriage. Anything outside of that is a perversion of His plan and purpose, and leads to atrocities like abortion, rape, sex trafficking, pornography, and much more. God created sex and the pleasures that come with it and put boundaries around it–not only because He has the right to do so, but because it's the best thing for us. It's been said that sex is like fire: within the confines of a fireplace, it provides warmth, pleasure, and beauty. Outside the fireplace, it will burn your house down.

It's very simple: The Bible is absolutely clear that all sex outside of marriage is a form of adultery, and adultery is sin.

THE STATS

The latest statistics and reports not only reveal the widespread viewing of porn but also the devastating consequences psychologically, physically, and spiritually.

Here are some stats from 2015 - 2018[5]:

- Forty-three percent (43%) of all internet users watch porn.
- Every second, over 28,000 internet users watch a pornographic video.
- Worldwide porn revenue is over $100B industry.
- Eighty-eight percent (88%) of scenes in porn films contain acts of physical aggression.
- Ninety percent (90%) of teens and ninety-six percent (96%) of young adults are either encouraging, accepting, or neutral when they talk about porn with their friends.

---

[5]"Porn Stats," *Covenant Eyes* (2018). Accessed December 10, 2021. www.covenanteyes.com/pornstats/

- One in five (20%) youth pastors and one in seven (14%) senior pastors use porn on a regular basis.
- Nearly twenty-seven percent (27%) of teens receive sexts.
- Fifty-one percent (51%) of male students and thirty-two percent (32%) of female students first viewed porn before their teenage years.
- Seventy-one percent (71%) of teens hide online behavior from their parents.
- Every day over 2.5 billion pornographic emails are sent.
- One in five (20%) mobile searches are for pornography.
- Virtual-reality porn is expected to top $1 *billion* by 2025.

SCIENCE AND THE DEVASTATING FACTS

The truth is, porn is everywhere, and affects millions of people all over the world in destructive ways. The scientific data pertaining to porn use is also alarming. Many people are truly addicted, as if they were taking a narcotic they can't quit. Donald J. Hilton, Jr., in an article written in summer 2010, said this: "In the case of narcotic addiction, the addicted person must increase the amount of the drug to get the same high. In pornography addiction, progressively more shocking images are required to stimulate the person." You can see where this can lead and how destructive it can be for watchers of porn and for society. One of the most devastating results of porn consumption is that it makes intimacy meaningless and robs people of love and intimacy. John D. Martin writes:

> The soul also notices the difference between virtual sex and real romantic and erotic relationships. Studies of internet pornography use have indicated a link between porn use and various negative effects on one's mental health and personal relationships, including depression and social isolation. At least sixteen states have formally recognized the growing use of pornography as a public health crisis and are pushing for legislative measures to combat the widespread dissemination of porn via the internet.
>
> Because it engenders progeny, sex has the greatest long-term consequences of all human acts in the natural order, and it there-

> fore has profound meaning. Pornography, however, by nature reduces sex to auto-eroticism, eliminating any possibility that the real meaning of sexuality will be realized. There is already considerable evidence that porn use is a factor in declining sex drives, especially among men, and it is therefore also a factor in declining fertility in countries where it is widespread.[6]

Since porn use contributes to a loss of meaning, it is not surprising that it is also linked to mental disorders such as depression. Consumption of pornography divorces sexual pleasure from its real purpose, and the soul notices.

Consumption of pornography divorces sexual pleasure from its real purpose, and the soul notices.

According to the Fight the New Drug website: "Decades of studies from respected institutions have demonstrated significant impacts of porn consumption for individuals, relationships, and society. Porn can impact self-esteem, relationship satisfaction, men's ability to be aroused, what turns a person on, sexual health, mental health, friendships, rates of sexual assault, the brain, feelings of shame, sex trafficking, friendships, and body image."[7]

CONCLUSION

To be clear, both pornography itself and the act of watching it is considered sin to God. It not only wreaks havoc on individuals and society, but many of the people (especially females) within the porn industry are forced to engage in sexual practices against their will, which means if you watch, you are part of the problem. Pornography is a big deal and the above is evidence enough to show why it is "so wrong."

---

[6]John D. Martin, "Three False Paths That Will Lead You Astray," *Salvo Magazine* 56, Spring 2021. https://salvomag.com/article/salvo56/our-search-for-meaning

[7]"Get the Facts," *Fight the New Drug*. Accessed December 10, 2021. www.fightthenewdrug.org/get-the-facts/

GET HELP

If you are a parent, ask your kids if they have watched porn and take steps to help them. If you, as a parent or an adult, struggle with porn, please get help.

Pure Life Ministries
purelifeministries.org

Operation Integrity
operationintegrity.org
Email: info@operationintegrity.org

Fight The New Drug
fightthenewdrug.org

Covenant Eyes
Covenanteyes.com

Chapter 4

HOW DID WE GET SO MANY RACES OF PEOPLE?

D. Marc Jacobs, Jr., and Carl Kerby

If we're honest, racism is sadly still an issue in our world today. You can't get away from the anger, bitterness, and strife that we see from groups on all sides of this issue. The following examples are ones that I (Carl) have heard or experienced over the years from churchgoing, "Bible-believing" Christians!

- "God separated the 'races' and now you're trying to put them back together!"
- "Robins breed with robins and blue jays breed with blue jays. That's how it (should be) with humans."
- "You're just trying to justify your sin!"
- I've had churches cancel speaking events for me because they found out that my wife was Japanese. One pastor told me, *"Our church bylaws state that if I let a man in*

an interracial marriage speak in my pulpit, I'll be removed from ministry."

- Or how about the deacon who ashamedly admitted to me that one of his responsibilities was to inform anyone who attended their service and had a different skin tone that they may feel more comfortable attending a different church the next week?
- Or how about my own grandmother who saw her great-grandchildren only twice in their lifetime because "they (have) *those* eyes." I could go on, but for the sake of brevity, I won't.

So, how do we deal with the issue of race? Should we even deal with it? Should we just let "sleeping dogs lie?" Well, this dog ain't sleeping; in fact, it's rabid! It needs to be put down for good, and there's only one way to do it … biblically! God's Word is where those of us who claim Christ as our Savior need to turn in order to deal with this as well as any other issue that arises. I believe one of the first steps in dealing with this sensitive topic is to understand where "races" came from. We'll look at it first in God's Word, then we'll see how science confirms the Bible.

WHAT DOES THE BIBLE SAY?

The Bible makes it abundantly clear that we ALL go back to one man, Adam (1 Corinthians 15:45), and one woman, Eve (Genesis 3:20). That means there's only ONE RACE–the human race. Yes, there are tribes and nations, which we'll talk about, but there's only one "race" of people. As a matter of fact, the Bible never talks about "races" when speaking of His created beings; the word "races" is only used in the context of "running a race." So, how did we get here from there? I believe the easiest way to explain the different genetic traits that we see in the human population today is from the biblical account of the Tower of Babel.

After the flood, the descendants of Noah and his sons gathered in one place (Genesis 11:1,2). The problem was, God had commanded people to spread out and inhabit the whole Earth (Genesis 1:28; 9:7). Because of their disobedience, God confused their central language

(Genesis 11:7). This has had a profound impact on humans to this day. One obvious result was that mankind began to spread out, as they had originally been commanded to do. The dispersion from Babel as depicted in the compiled historical journals of the Genesis account offer remarkable context not only to the world's languages, but also to the physical features that distinguish the world's variety of people groups.

Imagine if Adam and Eve were not "white" or "black." To do so, you first need to understand that no one is truly "white" or "black." Every human has the same skin *color*; it's opaque. Unless you're an albino, we're all lighter or darker shades of brown. This is due to two things: a pigment called melanin and specific genes that work together to give us our different tones.

Starting with a middle brown skin tone, it's very easy to show that it's possible for future human offspring to have a wide variety of shades of brown. As a matter of fact, I use numerous pictures (like the ones below) in my talks demonstrating that middle brown couples (or couples where one parent is "dark" and the other "light") can have twins where one is "light" and the other "dark." Our "color" is nothing more than a genetic trait influenced by environmental triggers! (Note: I even added a bonus picture to show the variation within my own family!)

I would suggest that Noah and his family members would probably have been middle brown. After the flood, as the human population started to increase in size, they would have continued to maintain this trait, since they all lived in the same environment.

When God confused their central language, this larger population broke into smaller groups who connected based on shared communication. Some of these groups would have moved off into different environments, as God had commanded them to do in the first place (Genesis 1:28). As families and tribes became isolated, the genetic potential for variation within these smaller groups narrowed. Distinct physical features were a product of genetically selected qualities that were prominently available and most environmentally suitable. Imagine middle brown people moving to hot, arid climates such as Africa. Over time, the genetic trait for the lightest skin tones would be lost, as this was pre-sunscreen time, and those folks would have died off in that environment.

WHAT DOES THE SCIENCE SAY?

Interestingly enough, this scenario is not exclusive to the biblical model of diversification; it is also supported by scientific study. In a March 2009, *Discover* magazine article entitled "Are We Still Evolving?"[8] Kathleen McAuliffe offers the following contribution from two DNA researchers from California:

> In our far-flung domains, humans presumably encountered starkly different selective forces as they adjusted to novel foods, predators, climates, and terrains.
>
> All … findings mesh beautifully with the notion that cultural and demographic shifts sparked our transformation. Our exodus out of Africa, for example, paved the way for one of the most obvious markers of race, skin hue.[9] As scientists widely

---

[8]Kathleen McAuliffe, "Are We Still Evolving?" *Discover*, March 2009, 51-58. http://www.astralgia.com/editing/clips/stillevolving2009.pdf

[9]Anne Habermehl, "Where in the World Is the Tower of Babel?" *Answers Research Journal* 4 (2011): 25-53. https://answersresearchjournal.org/where-is-the-tower-of-babel/. This reference to Africa indicates this is written from an evolutionary bias. The biblical account of the Tower of Babel is believed by consensus to have been in Mesopotamia, a region in southwestern Asia, not Africa at all.

> recognize, paler complexions are a genetic adjustment to low light: people with dark skin have trouble manufacturing vitamin D from ultraviolet radiation in northern latitudes, which makes them more susceptible to serious bone deformities. Consequently, Europeans and Asians over the past 20,000 years evolved *[Note: Genetically adapted]* lighter skin through two dozen different mutations that decrease production in the skin pigment melanin.
>
> Similarly, the gene for blue eyes codes for paler skin coloring in many vertebrates and hence have piggybacked along with lighter skin … Harvard University evolutionary biologist Pardis Sebati defends that view. "The immune system and skin interact directly with the outside world," she says. "They are our last line of defense." Based on the current evidence, she concludes, sunlight and pathogens were among the strongest selective forces, and skin and the immune system underwent the most dramatic change…As Harvard geneticist David Altshuler wrote in response to one of Sebati's articles, "It's reassuring that differences between the races seem to be mostly skin deep."

Creationists have been promoting this idea for a long time. We would say that all our variations can be traced back to a moment of divine dispersal from a genetic bottleneck a few hundred years after the Flood–**one which has no room for any notion of racial superiority.**

The idea that "Groups of people vary in appearance because their ancestors had different biological histories," as promoted by Steve Olson in his book, *Mapping Human History* (2003), is not only unscientific speculation, but it is convenient fodder for those who seek justification for their racism.

Just as I am quick to criticize the writings of many evolutionists and the racist implications that logically follow, I am compelled to give credit when their discovery has led them to biblically consistent conclusions.

Toward the end of her previously mentioned *Discover* magazine article, Kathleen McAuliffe includes the following from her interview with University of Wisconsin at Madison anthropologist, John Hawks.

We overcome "racism" by starting with the One who created us, loves us, died for us, and wants to spend eternity with us!

"Hawks responds that the best safeguard against bigotry is educating the public. He thinks we understand enough about human genetics to know that the notion of racial superiority is absurd. Intelligence, he argues, is not a single trait but a vast suite of abilities, and each ancestral environment may have favored a different set of talents. What is sorely needed, he says, is an 'ecological framework' to interpret the results. 'Groups are best adapted to their environment, which eliminates the question of superiority.'"

Beyond an ecological framework, what is sorely needed is a biblical framework from which every observation can be rightly interpreted.

CONCLUSION

The straightforward reading of Genesis represents a history that places all people groups on equal moral, spiritual, and intellectual footing. All of mankind, regardless of birthright, economic status, or academic training is accountable to a holy God for their fallen state. We're ALL sinners and each of us, regardless of what we look like on the outside, needs a Savior to rescue us from our sin. Every man and woman must personally look to the Creator's provision for restoration–the Scripture's prophesied, typified, and revealed Savior of humanity (and ultimately of all of creation), Jesus Christ. We overcome "racism" by starting with the One who created us, loves us, died for us, and wants to spend eternity with us!

Chapter 5

WHY IS ABORTION WRONG IF GOD ALLOWS US TO CHOOSE?

DR. DAVID ROSS

To answer this complex question, let's break it down into two components. First, "Is abortion wrong and why?" Second, "Are there any limits to the free choice God has given us?" We'll begin with the latter question on choice.

ARE THERE ANY LIMITS TO THE CHOICE GOD HAS GIVEN US?

Let's go back to the very beginning of recorded history found in the book of Genesis. This first book of the Bible explains how God created the universe and all things in it, including the very first human beings, Adam and Eve. They were created and placed in a wonderful garden where they could spend their days enjoying an intimate relationship with God, God's creation, and each other in perfect harmony and fellowship. According to Genesis 1:27, both Adam and Eve were created in God's image. This means that they were given the capacity to exercise freedom in making decisions and had the ability to choose right or wrong.

God also created what we know as the moral law by which the universe operates. Moral law is based on what *God* says is right and wrong. We see that God explained to Adam and Eve that doing good meant following what God said was good, and that doing wrong (or evil) was going against God's instructions. It turns out that God gave Adam, and by extension Eve, only one prohibited behavior: *Do not eat from the tree of the knowledge of good and evil* (Genesis 2:16). God told Adam and Eve to enjoy themselves, to cultivate the garden, and to not eat from one specific tree.

What we see from the very beginning is that, despite God having given humans free choice, it did not mean that all choices were equal or okay. Rather, only those choices that follow what God desires can be called good while all others are considered bad or evil. In fact, the rest of the Bible often uses the term "sin" for choices that people make that are bad or evil as they are in opposition to what God desires and has commanded. Therefore, we can sum things up like this: *God has given us freedom to choose, but not every choice we make is good.* Only those choices that align with what God desires can be considered good.

IS ABORTION WRONG AND WHY?

Now that we have established that our freedom to choose has limits, let's take a look at that first question to see what God said about abortion. God has given us His commands through the Bible; thus, it serves as a guide to what God considers good or evil. To understand God's position on abortion, we will need to understand what abortion actually involves.

Only those choices that align with what God desires can be considered good.

According to Merriam-Webster's dictionary, abortion is "*the intentional termination of a human pregnancy after, accompanied by, resulting in, or closely followed by the death of the embryo.*" To justify their stance, some have debated as to when a human embryo becomes human. However, modern science reveals that a human embryo becomes human at the point of conception, and this is when a unique living human being is created.[10] This tiny human needs nothing more than time, air, water, and food to continue developing into a larger person who eventually will be born, then grow into adulthood.

We now know that the developing child is not an extension of the mother's body, but rather contains a completely distinct set of DNA, which was formed at the moment of conception. The child's DNA remains distinct throughout the entirety of his life. So, to paraphrase the definition of abortion, we can say that abortion is the killing of a human being at some point between conception and birth. Naturally, since this human being has not yet been born, they are innocent of all wrongdoing and thus not deserving of death.

What we see throughout the Bible is that God says that killing innocent people is wrong, and, in fact, constitutes a prohibited, murderous act.

Now that we know what abortion is (the killing of an innocent human being), we can determine what God has to say about killing innocent human beings. In Exodus 20:13, God says: "You shall not murder." Then, in Proverbs 6:16-17, God says that He hates the killing of innocent people. What we see throughout the Bible is that God says that killing innocent people is wrong, and, in fact, constitutes a prohibited, murderous act. This fact is so established in the human conscience that nearly every culture in the world also understands that killing an innocent person is wrong.

Given that abortion kills an innocent human being, we can conclude that abortion is wrong. Additionally, anyone who has had an abortion, encouraged an abortion, or performed an abortion is committing evil or sin in God's eyes, as they are participating in the murder of an innocent person.

CONCLUSION

Is there hope for me if I've had an abortion?

We have seen that if a woman is pregnant, abortion is not an

---

[10]An example of what modern science has had to admit can be read in the following article. Ivy Nichols, "When is a Fetus a Human Being?" *Point of View*, September 13, 2021). https://pointofview.net/articles/when-is-a-fetus-a-human-being/

option as it kills an innocent human being. But what about all the women who have already had an abortion? Is there any hope for them to ever be forgiven by God?

Many people who have had or been involved in having an abortion find themselves asking this question. Often, after an abortion, the mother as well as the father of the baby feel shame, guilt, and sadness, which is the natural response when we disobey God or choose to sin. Sadly, many people are so overcome with guilt and shame that they feel they are beyond forgiveness and that God could never love them after what they have done.

As mentioned earlier, God gave us the Bible so we would understand Him better, as well as understand what He wants us to do with our lives. The Bible details the story of a person who at one point in his life was known for his murderous ways. His name was Saul of Tarsus, and he was a leader in the Jewish community. During the time of the early church, he went around imprisoning and killing people who chose to follow Jesus.

One day, while Saul was traveling to another city to find more people to imprison and put to death, God stopped him on the road and spoke to him. God explained that what Saul was doing was wrong, and Saul realized that he needed to repent (which means to turn from his sinful ways) and turn back to doing what God desired. Saul learned from God that *he* could be forgiven for all he had done if he put his faith in Jesus, the Son of God (Acts 9). After this event, Saul put his faith in Jesus and began sharing the message that even the worst sinners, like himself, could find forgiveness through faith in Jesus. It was during this time that Saul took on his new name, which you likely are more familiar with, and became known as Paul the Apostle (Acts 13:9).

This hope is found in a relationship with Jesus, who has made God's love and forgiveness available to all who trust in Him.

Learning about the Apostle Paul should give us all hope, especially those of us who have participated in an abortion. We learn that God still loves us and wants us to repent. He wants us to turn from our sinful, evil ways and trust in Jesus so we can receive the forgiveness that only He can provide. In fact, if we trust in Jesus, we will be given a new life–which is what happened with Paul.

Paul went on to write about his experience with God in the book of Romans so that other people would understand the forgiveness and hope found in Jesus. Paul said that although we all have sinned and fall short of God's standard for how we are to behave, God still loves us and sent His Son Jesus to die on a cross, taking on the penalty for our sin. Peace with God and eternal salvation is available to everyone who trusts in Jesus as the one who paid for their sins and who asks for God's forgiveness. In fact, God promises that those who trust in Jesus will never be condemned, no matter how bad their past behavior has been (Romans 3:23-24; 5:1,8,13; 8:1).

These verses offer much hope for all who have had abortions. This hope is found in a relationship with Jesus, who has made God's love and forgiveness available to all who trust in Him.

Chapter 6

WHAT ABOUT ALIENS?

DAN LIETHA

Many people ask the question, "Are we alone in the universe?" In fact, there are quite a few reasons why you may be asking it as well. Space aliens are everywhere in our entertainment. Of the top ten highest grossing movies of all time, half of them feature space aliens.[11] Aliens are not only in movies but also in TV shows, books, comic books, commercials, toys, t-shirts, and on and on. From Kryptonians to Vulcans, Klingons to Wookies, our minds are filled with the idea of space aliens daily. These are all fictional characters, but they still influence our thinking.

If we look at the real world of science, we can see billions of dollars being spent on telescopes, satellites, space probes, and other space vehicles to explore planets and the heavens in search of life beyond Earth. The SETI (Search for Extraterrestrial Intelligence) Institute is an organization of scientists that are looking for signals and signs of alien

[11]Nate Millado, "100 Highest-grossing Movies of all Time," *Parade*, October 5, 2021. https://parade.com/1099666/nate-millado/highest-grossing-movies-all-time/

life, as well as sending signals into space to contact possible life forms that may be out there somewhere.[12] And recently, the US government has formed the Unidentified Aerial Phenomena (UAP) Task Force. The purpose of this program within the United States Office of Naval Intelligence is to "standardize collection and reporting"[13] on sightings of unexplained aerial vehicles (UFOs). If some of the smartest people on the planet are going to such lengths to search for alien life, it must be out there, right?

WHY SOME THINK ALIEN LIFE IS POSSIBLE

Time, space, and matter are the three main qualities of the universe that are referenced as reasons for the possibility of life beyond our planet. Many believe that billions of years of time brought life into existence on Earth, so if it happened here, why not somewhere else in this massive universe?

When Carl Sagan, a well-known evolutionist, was asked if he thought there may be some sort of intelligence out there, his response was as follows:

> May, surely may. We now realize an enormous number of planets. A range of planetary systems around the nearby stars. So, there's a lot of potential abodes for it. That's one thing. Then the question of organic matter. The carbon-rich complex molecules that are essential for the kind of life we know about are fantastically abundant, they litter the universe. We see them in asteroids and in comets. In the moons, in the outer solar system. And even in the cold dark spaces between the stars. The stuff of life is everywhere. And then there's time. There are billions of years for biological evolution on all those worlds. There are many worlds that are much older than ours. So, you put those together, lots of places, lots of organic matter, and lots of time; it seems very hard to believe that our paltry little planet is the only one that's inhabited.[14]

---

[12]Go to www.seti.org for more information.

[13]Intelligence Authorization Act for Fiscal Year 2021, S. Rep. No. 116-233 (2020). https://www.govinfo.gov/content/pkg/CRPT-116srpt233/pdf/CRPT-116srpt233.pdf

[14]Carl Sagan on October 4, 1985, as told to Studs Terkel. The WFMT Studs Terkel Radio Archive. https://www.youtube.com/watch?v=u9WHs49nlHk

WHAT DOES THE BIBLE SAY?

The Bible is God's Word to us. It instructs us not only in spiritual things, but also in earthly things. Our Creator tells us how He brought the universe into existence. Though Scripture does not deal directly with the topic of alien life, there are facts and clues in Scripture that help us answer the question of their possible existence. As we look to the creation account, as well as other related parts of Scripture, let's consider some helpful and important questions:

1. What was God's purpose in creating the universe?
2. What is man's place and purpose in the universe?

THE CREATION ACCOUNT

The Bible clearly states that God created the universe in six, 24-hour, Earth rotation days (Genesis 1). By looking at the numbers given in the Biblical genealogies from the first man, Adam, to Abraham (2,000 years), Abraham to Christ (2,000 years), and Christ to our present day (2,000 years), the age of the Earth adds up to be around 6,000 years. There are many other lines of evidence that confirm this time span for the universe's duration. This is nowhere near the 13.8-billion-year-old universe that evolutionary scientists currently claim.[15] The essential time factor (claimed as necessary for aliens to evolve) is not in Scripture.

But what if God *created* alien life during the six days of creation? Does the Bible deal with that possibility? To answer this question, we return to the order of events in the creation week in Genesis 1.

On Day 1 (Genesis 1:1-5), the Earth is the first object created in the entire universe. That makes it the oldest object in the universe! And it remained the lone object in the entire universe until creation Day 4. This gives us a hint about the priority and purpose God places on the Earth in relation to the rest of the universe.

On Day 4 (Genesis 1:14-19), the rest of the universe is given attention with the creation of the sun, moon, stars, planets, and other celestial objects.

---

[15] Doyle Rice, "Universe is 13.8 billion years old, scientists confirm," *USA Today*, July 15, 2020. https://www.usatoday.com/story/news/nation/2020/07/15/age-universe-13-8-billion-years-scientists-confirm/3287409001/

> And God said, "Let there be lights in the expanse of the heavens to separate the day from the night. And let them be for signs and for seasons, and for days and years, and let them be lights in the expanse of the heavens to give light upon the earth." And it was so. And God made the two great lights—the greater light to rule the day and the lesser light to rule the night—and the stars. And God set them in the expanse of the heavens to give light on the earth, to rule over the day and over the night, and to separate the light from the darkness. And God saw that it was good. And there was evening and there was morning, the fourth day.

Notice that even though the celestial objects are beyond the Earth, they still have a connection to Earth. Their purpose is "for signs and for seasons" on Earth.

If God created alien life, Day 4 would be the day for it, as all the other days of creation deal with the Earth. But at this point in creation, the only life on Earth are the plants created on Day 3 and, biblically, they are not considered life. It seems out of place that God would create alien civilizations on this day when He has yet to create the animals and, more importantly, man and woman on Earth. Why would He create some other beings when the beings He is so focused on have yet to be created?

Humans are the pinnacle of God's creation, because we alone are created in the image of God.

On Days 5 and 6, God created life on Earth, and His final and best creation are the first two humans on Day 6. Humans are the pinnacle of God's creation, because we alone are created in the image of God. "Then God said, 'Let us make man in our image, after our likeness…' So, God created man in his own image, in the image of God he created him; male and female he created them" (Genesis 1:26-27). We see that the focus of scriptural revelation is on Earth and the center of that focus is mankind.

THE FALL OF MAN AND THE CORRUPTION OF THE ENTIRE UNIVERSE

The universe was created perfect by our perfect Creator, and He concluded His creation by proclaiming it "very good" in Genesis 1:31. Originally there was no death or suffering because there was no sin. Sadly, it didn't take long for Adam and Eve to disobey their Creator. This first human sin brought judgment and corruption onto not only the Earth, but the entire creation. "For we know that the whole creation has been groaning together in the pains of childbirth until now" (Romans 8:22).

God's "very good" creation is not very good anymore, and that is because of something that happened on this one tiny blue dot in the universe that we know as Earth. You see, Earth is the key to the rest of the universe. As far as God's attention goes to His Creation, Earth is the center of it. If there were Vulcans and Kryptonians on other planets, does it seem right that they would be cursed because of something that happened on some other planet that is galaxies away from them?

The animal kingdom and even the Earth itself was given to man and placed under his dominion. Even though they did not sin, the curse affected them because they were placed under man's dominion. In fact, even though none of *us* were in the Garden of Eden to sin along with Adam, we are part of that sin because we are related to Adam. "Therefore, just as sin came into the world through one man, and death through sin, and so death spread to all men because all sinned" (Romans 5:12). The same could not be said for any alien life, so why would they suffer for what happened on Earth?

THE HOPE OF A UNIVERSE RESTORED

Not only was the universe ruined because of man's sin on Earth, but the promise of a future restoration of the entire universe was also made on Earth. In Genesis 3:15, as God was pronouncing the curse on His creation, we see the glorious first promise of a coming Savior. "I will put enmity between you and the woman, and between your offspring and her offspring; he shall bruise your head, and you shall bruise his heel" (Genesis 3:15). The Creator kept His promise and came to Earth some 4,000 years later to accomplish this heavenly task.

Galatians 4:4-7 (NASB)

> But when the fullness of the time came, God sent forth His Son, born of a woman, born under the Law, so that He might redeem those who were under the Law, that we might receive the adoption as sons. Because you are sons, God has sent forth the Spirit of His Son into our hearts, crying, "Abba! Father!" Therefore you are no longer a slave, but a son; and if a son, then an heir through God.

He came to the first and oldest planet in the universe, Earth, to pay for man's sin debt that had ruined the universe. The good news that Jesus came to earth to die for the sins of mankind is great news for us, but for Vulcans and Kryptonians it would be very bad news. You see, only members of the human race have the possibility of a restored relationship with the Creator.

1 Corinthians 15:22,45,47,49

> For as in Adam all die, so also in Christ shall all be made alive … Thus, it is written, "The first man, Adam, became a living being"; the last Adam became a life-giving spirit … The first man [Adam] was from the Earth, a man of dust; the second man [Jesus] is from heaven … Just as we have borne the image of the man of dust, we shall also bear the image of the man of heaven.

Any aliens that would be elsewhere in the universe would not be included in this salvation and restoration. They would have no hope.

FALSE HOPE IN ALIEN LIFE

Why are so many looking to the heavens for other beings? They are searching for something beyond what we have on earth, because they want answers for life and cures for diseases. They want to live in a world that is free of suffering and death. In short, they are looking for a replacement for God. The truth is, everyone longs to see the broken things in our world restored to perfection. Thankfully, all this brokenness will eventually come to an end, and the perfect creation will be restored, but it won't be at the hands of space aliens. Only the One who created the universe, Jesus Christ, can restore it.

Revelation 21:1-5

> Then I saw a new heaven and a new earth, for the first heaven and the first earth had passed away, and the sea was no more. And I saw the holy city, New Jerusalem, coming down out of heaven from God, prepared as a bride adorned for her husband. And I heard a loud voice from the throne saying, "Behold, the dwelling place of God is with man. He will dwell with them, and they will be his people, and God himself will be with them as their God. He will wipe away every tear from their eyes, and death shall be no more, neither shall there be mourning, nor crying, nor pain anymore, for the former things have passed away. And he who was seated on the throne said, "Behold, I am making all things new." Also, he said, "Write this down, for these words are trustworthy and true."

CONCLUSION

We began by asking, "What about aliens?" The Bible answers decisively against the possibility of alien life evolving over billions of years by indicating a very young universe that is not old enough to accommodate the eons of time that evolutionists demand.

Then we asked the question, "What if God *created* life somewhere beyond the Earth?" Since the focus of Scripture is on the Earth and God's relationship to man, it doesn't clearly state that life does not exist outside of the Earth.

The lack of specifics in Scripture on possible life elsewhere seems to hinder our ability to be dogmatic in answering this question; however, the high priority and focus that Scripture has on Earth and mankind provide a much stronger case against the existence of any intelligent life or civilizations beyond Earth. Earth is clearly the beginning of God's creation and was created to be the home for His highest creation, the *only* creation created in His image, the human race. The Earth also became the point of ruin for the entire universe and the place where hope for a new universe comes from. The Bible doesn't address the issue because it's irrelevant to its central theme: the redemption of man.

PART TWO

REFUTING EVOLUTION

Chapter 7

HOW DO WE KNOW WHAT IS REAL AND WHAT IS FAKE?

JUAN VALDES

I have been the proud owner of three Rolex watches purchased for $20 each in the streets of Manhattan. My claim to fame is twofold. Not too many people can say they have owned three Rolex watches, and not too many people can say they have bought them at a better price. The one disclaimer is that they work for about two weeks, then they stop working forever. Why is that? Well, I guess you can figure that out—they are fake. Whether we are buying a Rolex, diamonds, gold coins, or artwork, authenticity is really important. Why? Well, the value of what we acquire is directly proportional to its authenticity. The price of a cubic zirconia (fake diamond) is quite different from the value of a real diamond. So, how does this apply to our walk as Christians?

Nowhere is authenticity more important than in the life of a Christian. Let's consider two specific areas of authenticity when it comes to our faith.

- First, we must concern ourselves with the authenticity of truth claims. In a world of so much confusion, so many contradicting truth claims, and so many false teachings, it is imperative to be able to distinguish between what is true and what is false.
- Second, authenticity with regards to people is of utmost importance. There are so many false teachers, false prophets, and fake Christians, we must be able to differentiate between those who are real and those who are not. It's also important to separate the two categories because the methods of evaluating them are different.

AUTHENTIC TRUTH CLAIMS

When it comes to truth claims, there are two important factors to consider.

First, we must consider the source of the claim. When evaluating claims such as "the Bible is full of errors and contradictions" or "Christians are hypocrites," it is wise to consider the source of the claim. When an atheist or an agnostic makes a claim about the Christian faith, special care should be taken to demand of them the basis for such a claim. We should ask them how they came to that conclusion? What arguments do they have in support of such a conclusion?

Usually, outsiders lack a deep understanding of the Christian faith and are therefore reaching conclusions prematurely without duly considering the facts. After all, we cannot expect someone on the outside to have spent significant time studying the Bible, theology, etc. It may surprise you how often people make such claims without any type of support. They make the claim but have never really thought about why they believe that to be the case. It's often something they have heard or read about, and they just adopt the idea and repeat it—you might call it recycled ignorance.

Nevertheless, sometimes people do spend time considering their position and are willing to present arguments in support of it. We owe it to ourselves and to the person making the claim to give the arguments full consideration. However, my experience is that the arguments presented are typically easy to debunk. But what if the source is a former Christian or a current Christian who is doubting their faith?

Undoubtedly, sometimes skepticism surfaces among Christians as well. Whether they still consider themselves Christian or whether they have walked away from their faith, these arguments carry much more weight. That is because we suppose the Christian has looked deeply into these issues and has found a genuine problem. It is still a good idea to ask the person making the claim to defend it. The same questions should be posed: Why do you believe that? How did you come to that conclusion? If in fact the claims are well thought out, it may require a bit more diligence on our behalf to evaluate the arguments. What we must never forget is that the truth is knowable (John 8:32), and when someone makes a claim contrary to the truth, an error in reasoning has occurred.

What about truth claims from the Bible? What is the source of these claims? How do we know if they are real or fake? As Christians, we know that the Bible is God's revelation to mankind. Therefore, truth claims in the Bible, when properly understood, are always true. How do we know? Because God is all-knowing (Psalm 139), and God does not lie (Hebrews 6:18). Some may question whether the Bible is in fact God's Word, and that is something we should be prepared to defend as well, so we will tackle it next.

What we must never forget is that the truth is knowable (John 8:32), and when someone makes a claim contrary to the truth, an error in reasoning has occurred.

The second factor is that we must consider the claim itself. Independently of the source, truth claims should be considered on their own merits. The most important question to ask ourselves is, does the truth claim correspond with reality? For example, let's consider the claim that "the Bible is God's Word." How do we know if that is true or false? Entire books have been written in response to this question, but let's look at one line of evidence that supports this truth claim.

A book that is the product of human intellect cannot predict the future with the level of detail found in the Bible. Sure, anyone can predict that tomorrow we will see a sunrise and a sunset, but can you predict the winning numbers of next week's lottery? Of course not. The Bible makes some amazing predictions, technically called prophecies, about future events. The level of detail and the rate of fulfillment (100%) is unparalleled in anything ever written. For example, there are over 100 detailed prophecies concerning the birth, life, death, and resurrection of Jesus[16] that have come true precisely as predicted. These prophecies are dated from a few hundred years to over a thousand years prior to their fulfilment. This is solid evidence in favor of the claim that the Bible is not the product of human intellect; it is the Word of God.

Having established that the Bible is the Word of God, it is the primary tool we should use when evaluating truth claims. If we are trying to figure out whether a claim is real or fake (true or false), we should first ask ourselves if the Bible has anything to say about the claim. If not, then we should proceed to test the claim using other tools at our disposal. However, it is my experience that most claims that sow doubt in our faith can be tested by considering what the Word of God says. But what about people? How do we know *who* is real and *who* is fake?

AUTHENTIC CHRISTIANS

When judging people, faulty expectations can often keep us from the truth. If perfection is part of our expectations for an "authentic Christian," then we will never, ever find one that meets our expectations. If failure or sin are considered signs of a "fake Christian," we will find that we are all fake. Jesus was the only sinless, perfect man to ever walk the Earth. Thus, we must be realistic in our expectations. Too often, we label people as hypocrites by appealing to a standard that would place all of humanity in that category as well. A Christian who sins is not necessarily a hypocrite. A true hypocrite is one who does not believe but pretends to be a Christian, nonetheless. Thus, we should be careful to define our terms and expectations based on reality as it is described in God's Word. The Word of God clearly teaches that nobody is good—not even one person—we have all sinned and fallen short of the glory of God (Romans 3:10,23). What then is an authentic Christian? How can we tell the difference between a "real" Christian and a "fake" Christian?

---

[16]J. Barton Payne, *Encyclopedia of Biblical Prophecy* (New York: Harper & Row, 1973), 147. He estimates 127 personal messianic predictions fulfilled in Jesus.

The key to determining who is a real follower of Jesus Christ and who is not was given to us by Jesus Himself. In Matthew 7, as part of the Sermon on the Mount, Jesus establishes a test for authenticity. Twice He says, "You will recognize them by their fruits" (Matthew 7:16,20). Interestingly, Jesus is quick to point out that we are not to be judged by what we *say*, but rather by what we *do*. Immediately after establishing this test of authenticity, Jesus pronounces one of the most sobering affirmations ever made, "Not everyone who says to me, 'Lord, Lord,' will enter the kingdom of heaven, but the one who does the will of my Father who is in heaven" (Matthew 7:21). The cliché seems to be on point—actions speak louder than words! Jesus also clarifies what good fruit looks like: "...the one who does the will of my Father..." These are the principles that Jesus Himself established to help us identify who is a real disciple and who is not. It is not perfection or sinlessness that point to our authenticity, but rather our commitment to obeying the will of God—even if we fall short in the day-to-day execution of that will.

CONCLUSION

The importance of being able to distinguish between real and fake Christians or true and false truth claims is of utmost importance. In both categories, the Bible is the common denominator. The Word of God helps us filter truth claims and identify what is true and what is false. The Word of God also gives us the parameters for judging between real and fake Christians. Thus, we need to know the Word of God, and we need to live by the Word of God, lest we too find ourselves in the wrong category. I encourage you to further enrich your knowledge on this topic by reading the next chapter, "How do you know something is true with absolute certainty if you haven't witnessed it?"

Chapter 8

HOW DO YOU KNOW SOMETHING IS TRUE WITH ABSOLUTE CERTAINTY IF YOU HAVEN'T WITNESSED IT?

JUAN VALDES

Scaling "Mount Knowledge" is indeed a difficult task. Most of us begin the long hike out of the "Valley of Ignorance" blissfully unconscious of our own ignorance. Ironically, in the valley of the unconsciously ignorant, we find some of the most eloquent ultracrepidarians (a cool new word I just learned that means: *people who love to express opinions about things they know absolutely nothing about*). Social media is inundated with many such unconsciously ignorant "experts." Because these "experts" present us with an almost infinite supply of contradicting positions and affirmations, it's easy to see why we are often left wondering if anything can be known with absolute certainty.

The "Valley of Ignorance" is surrounded by what seems to be

an endless array of mountains of knowledge. Some have climbed as far as they could up "Mount Philosophy," while others are reaching ever higher up "Mount Psychology." This makes a very important yet often overlooked point—we can be knowledgeable experts in one discipline and completely incompetent in another. Furthermore, the whole endeavor of scaling "Mount Knowledge" is based on at least two foundational assumptions:

- First, we assume that there is "truth" to be learned. (There *is* a mountain to climb.)
- Second, we assume that this truth is accessible or knowable. (We can climb it.)

Unless we affirm both, nothing in our world would make any sense at all.

Our question, "How do you know something is true with absolute certainty if you have not witnessed it?" does not define what the "something" is. Considering the setting in which these questions were collected (teen summer camps), it is probably referring to knowledge of God's existence, or the existence of Heaven and Hell, or some other tenet of the faith that lies in the realm of the physically unseen. For example, if we plug in "God" as the object of knowledge, the question will read, "How do you know *God exists* with absolute certainty if you haven't (seen Him)?" If we plug in "Heaven" as the object of knowledge, the question will read, "How do you know *Heaven exists* with absolute certainty if you haven't witnessed it?" To respond to these questions, we must first define "truth." Just as importantly, we must define "knowledge" and consider how we go about acquiring it. Finally, we need to deal with the relationship between knowledge and "absolute certainty." Is it possible for *anything* to be known with absolute certainty?

WHAT IS TRUTH?

To know whether something is true or not, we must first define what we mean by *truth*. A good working definition of truth is: "that which corresponds with reality." Something is *true* if it corresponds with the way things really are, and false if it does not. If I claim that there are twenty-five steps between the first and second floors of my church, how would you know if it is true?

Applying the definition above, you would physically count the steps as you climb from the first to the second floor. There happens to be exactly twenty-five steps, thus my claim is true; if not, my claim would have been false. This type of "truth" is known as *objective truth*. The claim is true independent of any human desire, opinion, or preference. We may *desire* that there be only six steps—which would make the climb so much easier—but that desire has no bearing on the truth. We may believe twenty steps are far more prudent—but that too is irrelevant. We may hate the number twenty-five, and again that would have no bearing on the truth. Bottom line–if we had never been born and had no opinion at all, there would still be twenty-five steps between the first and second floors of my church.

HOW DO WE KNOW IF SOMETHING IS TRUE?

While some may argue that knowledge about the real world is impossible, they are arguing that they KNOW this to be true, thus their argument is self-defeating. Truth about the real world is knowable. Consider the truth claim: *The God of the Bible exists*. Because this is an objective truth claim, our desires, preferences, and opinions have no bearing on whether it's true or not. Either God's existence corresponds with reality, or it doesn't. However, this is where it gets interesting. Unlike the simple process of counting steps, verifying the truthfulness of this claim is a bit more complicated, especially because God is the type of being that we don't "witness" in the traditional sense of the word. So, is there a way to "test" these types of claims to see if they are true? Of course.

There are three common "tests" we should be familiar with when we seek to find truth.

- The first we already alluded to above—the ***Test of Correspondence***. By physically counting the steps, we were able to verify the truthfulness of the claim. But sometimes the claim being considered does not allow for a test of correspondence. What then?
- The second test of truth is known as the ***Test of Coherence***. In cases where it is impossible to demonstrate correspondence between a claim and the reality it describes, we can test the claim's truth in terms

of how well it coheres with all other relevant information available to us. When we consider what we know about the universe we live in, everything points to the existence of a Creator that coincides with the God of the Bible.

  - There is design in the universe—therefore, there must be a divine Designer.
  - There is information in the universe—therefore, there must be a divine Informer.
  - There is objective morality in the universe—therefore, there must be a divine Legislator, etc.

- There is a third test that can sometimes be helpful in evaluating the veracity of some truth claims. The ***Test of Pragmatism*** comes in handy when we are evaluating worldviews in general. This test seeks to determine if an idea, truth claim, or worldview can be "lived" in everyday life. In other words, does it work? When evaluating the truth claim that all morality is relative (moral relativism), this test comes in handy, because we find that it is impossible to live out a morally relativistic philosophy of life. Even the most ardent moral relativist is only a relativist when it comes to the moral choices *they* make. However, if someone else chooses that it is morally acceptable to steal from them, their relativism goes out the door. In a truly relativistic world, we would have to respect the thief's moral choices as much as the rapist's and the molester's—after all, *everyone* decides for themselves what is right or wrong, and we can't judge them. Obviously, this idea fails the Test of Pragmatism.

These three tests are useful in *acquiring* knowledge, but we must also understand a bit more *about* knowledge.

When we ask if we can *know* something is true, we are asking if we are justified in believing it or not. If a claim passes all the appropriate tests, we can say that we are justified in believing that it is true. How do we know if we have exhausted all the appropriate tests for any given claim?

A simple way to know is when the *objections* to a claim carry more problems than the *belief in question*. Let's say I claim to be working in my church office. The Ring cameras show my car in the parking lot, and you call the church number and I answer. Also, several people confirm they saw me in the office at that time, so you are justified in believing that the claim is true. However, a skeptic may say that the car could be a hologram projected by an alien spacecraft, that I have someone imitating my voice in the office in order to trick you, *and* that I bribed several people to lie about my whereabouts. This is the kind of skepticism we often find ourselves engaged with. The skeptic's propositions are far more problematic than my claim. But please note that it is not necessary to be able to defend our claims against *any imaginable doubt*. All we need to do is be able to defend it against *any reasonable doubt*. This brings us to the topic of "absolute certainty."

WHAT ABOUT KNOWLEDGE WITH ABSOLUTE CERTAINTY?

Absolute certainty can be attained, but it has no bearing on whether something is true or not. Let me explain. The simplest definition of "certainty" is having no doubt about something. Adding "absolute" as a modifier serves to increase the level of belief to the highest possible level. When a person claims to have absolute certainty about something, they are saying that they believe there is no possible way for that belief to be false. For example, I am *absolutely certain* that the God of the Bible exists. But many atheists are *absolutely certain* that He does not exist. What this illustrates is that absolute certainty is achieved in our minds, but it doesn't necessarily establish that something is, in fact, true or false.

The certainty of our beliefs is only as valuable as the evidence we have to support it.

The certainty of our beliefs is only as valuable as the evidence we have to support it. A more important question is determining what we consider to be sufficient *knowledge* about a claim to believe it with absolute certainty in our minds. Speaking of sufficient knowledge requires us to break down the various ways of knowing things.

There are four main ways in which we come to know things.

- First, we accept many beliefs as being ***self-evidently true***. That is, to understand them is to know that they are true. Sometimes these claims are true due to the meaning of the words being used, also known as *analytic statements*. Claims such as "a circle is round" or "a bachelor is unmarried" are self-evident. The language itself establishes the truthfulness of the claims. Other things we accept as true fall under the category of *basic beliefs*. These beliefs are an integral part of every rational person's belief system. Truth claims like "I exist" or "there was a significant past" are true without any need to prove their veracity. Practically everyone knows these claims are true.

  Then there are things we come to know by *immediate sensory awareness*. These beliefs are based on personal experiences. When I have a headache, I know it because I'm immediately aware of it. All these ways of knowing fall under the category of self-evident knowledge and are usually accompanied by a high degree of certainty. Christians believe that God can be known in this way. Belief in God is basic to human beings. The fact of God's existence is at the very center of all other knowledge. In this sense, the nonexistence of God is something unthinkable, such as my nonexistence. However, when attempting to provide "proof" or "evidence" for God's existence to those who deny it, we must consider the other three ways in which we come to know things.

- A second way of acquiring knowledge is via our ***rationality***. Because human rationality is truly universal, it provides a common platform from which to address issues (such as God's existence) with unbelievers. From a rational perspective, a claim is believed to be true if it is logically deduced from an undisputed "given" starting point.

- For example, the law of causality is a universal given, meaning it is accepted by practically everyone. Everyone knows that all effects must have a cause. Without this universal "given," science would be impossible. That's why arguments from creation are particularly strong evidence for God's existence. Given that the universe began to exist (a fairly undisputed fact), it must have a cause outside of itself (the law of causality), and that points us in the direction of a supernatural creator—one that exists outside of the natural realm.

- The specific characteristics of the universe (also fairly undisputed) point us in the direction of a particular supernatural creator with a very specific set of attributes (via abductive reasoning), and the God of the Bible is the only proposed God that has the entire list of necessary characteristics.

- Furthermore, it can also be argued that a claim's rational credibility is further strengthened when counterclaims are irrational or incoherent, as is the claim that everything came from nothing.

• A third way in which we come to know things, which is also universal in nature, is via ***sensory information***. Much of our knowledge is rooted in sensory experience. This means that a belief is justified when it is a sound inference from a sensory observation. Because the data that our senses perceive must be processed, we speak of "observations," not just sensory impressions. This way of knowing is at the heart of the natural sciences.

- For example, something we observe rather abundantly is the presence of design in our universe. William Paley, an 18th century English philosopher and apologist, is known in part for his watchmaker analogy. In a nutshell, he argued that if we found a watch in the forest, we would never even consider the possibility that the watch simply grew in the forest. Our observations of the watch would inevitably point in the direction of a watchmaker. This argument appeals to the inherent improbability of something as complex as the universe simply having happened. Thus, the design that we observe in our universe seems to point in the direction of a supernatural Designer.

- The fourth and final way we come to know things is by practice or ***workability***. The idea here is that a belief is justified if it has practical consequences that are consistent with it.
    - For example, we can *believe* that we can ride a unicycle (something we have never done before), but unless we pass the test of practice, we don't really "know" that we can do it. The belief is not justified if it doesn't work.

CONCLUSION

When we pursue truth, certainty is only as useful as the way we come to know it. As we have seen, knowing something with "absolute certainty" doesn't really make it true. The nature of reality is such that something that *is* true does not require anyone to know or prove that it is true. It is true simply because it corresponds with reality, whether we can prove it or not and whether we know it or not. There is a difference between the way things *are* (reality) and whether they can be known or proven. In other words, the inability to prove that something is true to the satisfaction of others has no bearing on whether it is true or not. If you ask me to "prove" that I have a headache, I cannot prove it. That does not mean it's not true, it simply means that it is impossible for me to prove it to someone else.

So how do we come to know that the God of the Bible exists? How do we come to know that Heaven and Hell are real? We can use the faculties God has given us. We can test truth claims. We can come to know things in these various ways. However, there is also an answer key that we can use to check our answers to these tough questions—the Bible. God has not left it entirely up to us to find all truth—instead He has revealed THE truth in writing, in nature, and in person, so that we are without excuse (Romans 1:20).

God has not left it entirely up to us to find all truth—instead He has revealed THE truth in writing, in nature, and in person, so that we are without excuse (Romans 1:20).

Chapter 9

IF GOD MADE ADAM AND EVE IN THE BEGINNING, WHERE WERE THE DINOSAURS–WEREN'T THEY BEFORE THAT TIME?[17]

Juan Valdes & Carl Kerby

Playing fetch with a baby T-rex would have been a sight to see! Seriously, though, did man and dinosaurs really coexist? This question highlights the difference a worldview makes. We all have worldviews. That is, we all see the world through a particular set of lenses, which are shaped by the things we believe to be true of the world we live in. When it comes to origins, there are many opinions, beliefs, and arguments, but they all fall back on one of two distinct worldviews.

- On the one hand, you have the worldview of naturalism that believes all life forms evolved by natural unguided processes over billions of years without needing any

[17]If we were to "rank" the questions by how often they're asked, this would be in the Top 10! The world is still fascinated by dinosaurs, especially the younger generation.

"supernatural shenanigans" as atheist Lawrence Krauss likes to say.[18]

- On the other hand, you have the biblical worldview that presents a totally different perspective.

To deal with this question thoroughly, we need to consider the naturalist account of origins, particularly with regards to dinosaurs and man. Then, we need to consider the biblical account of what happened. Finally, we need to evaluate the evidence to see which perspective it really supports. So, let's begin with the "no-shenanigans" view.

WHAT DO NATURALISTS SAY?

"In the beginning, there was no god." That is the starting point of the naturalist story. Their entire story is built upon a foundation of no god, no design, no purpose–just natural selection responding to randomness in the material world. Let's glance at the highlights of the story. According to this story, there was an explosion some 13.8 billion years ago from which all the matter in the universe came forth. About 4.5 billion years ago, the sun, the Earth and the other planets of our solar system came together. Somehow, a billion years later (3.5 billion years ago) the first living cell appeared on Earth (note the word "**somehow**," because nobody in that camp has a clue as to the origins of the first cell, nor do they have a clue as to where the stuff that "banged" originally came from). That began a process by which a worm-like creature *over time* turned into a fish, which *over time* turned into an amphibian, which *over time* turned into a rat-like creature, which *over time* turned into a wolf-like creature, which *over time* went back into the ocean to become a blue whale! All of this, mind you, via naturalistic processes which are supposedly still happening today. And you thought it was Christians that have problems with their history!

The story also says that the amphibians eventually turned into dinosaurs, which are supposed to have arrived around 250 million years ago and lived until about sixty-five million years ago, when the last living dinosaurs became extinct. (Nobody really knows how or why that happened either.)

The first humans didn't appear on the scene until much later.

[18]Lawrence M. Krauss, "A Universe from Nothing," *Radcliffe Institute* (July 17, 2013). https://www.youtube.com/watch?v=vwzbU0bGOdc

The first bipedal hominids (our supposed oldest apelike ancestors) are believed to have walked the Earth around 4.4 million years ago. However, modern humans are a much more recent development. We first made our entrance some 250,000 years ago.[19] Whew! What a story! And that's just the animal kingdom—remember that all plant life evolved from that first living cell as well. That first living cell must have really been something!

For our intents and purposes, the most relevant portion of the timeline is that of dinosaurs and modern man. These two timelines don't overlap at all, not even close. (See illustration above.) The last dinosaur croaked at least sixty-one million years before the very first supposed apelike ancestor arrived, and almost sixty-five million years before modern man arrived. Therefore, from ***this*** perspective it is absolutely ludicrous to imply that man and dinosaurs coexisted, unless you're watching the Flintstones! But, what about the other perspective?

WHAT DOES GOD SAY?

"In the beginning, God!" That's the starting point of the biblical worldview. It's also important to note that this is God's perspective on *what* happened and *how* it happened. This history is built upon the foundation of an eternal, all-powerful, loving God, who is also the Creator of all things. God created the universe with purpose and design. According to this version, in the beginning, God created the heavens

---

[19]Please note that the dates listed above vary from source to source, because nobody really knows exactly when these purported events happened, but this represents the most widely accepted chronology in contemporary science.

and the Earth. Within a period of six, 24-hour days, God created everything. Large reptiles living in the oceans, as well as flying reptiles, were created on Day 5, while the land-dwelling dinosaurs were created on Day 6. You will hear the word "dinosaur" used for flying and marine reptiles, but this is **not** correct. They are not classified as dinosaurs. The word "dinosaur" only pertains to a very specific group of land-dwelling reptiles with very unique features. Mankind was also created on Day 6.

The dates for *when* these days occurred have been excluded because the Bible doesn't provide them specifically. However, using the genealogies and other contextual clues, it was **not** billions of years ago—it was only thousands (but we address the age of the Earth in the chapter entitled, "Is the Earth 415 million years old?" so we will not engage with it here).

From this perspective, there's no conflict whatsoever with the idea of man and dinosaur both inhabiting the Earth at the same time. There is, however, much conflict between the two versions of origins presented. They cannot both be true. Also, contrary to the belief of some people, they are irreconcilable.

- Either there is a God, or there isn't.
- Either the universe is designed, or it isn't.
- Either there's purpose behind our existence, or there isn't.
- Either the origins were guided, or they weren't.
- Either we all share a common ancestor, or we don't.
- Either man coexisted with dinosaurs, or he didn't.

How do we decide which version is true? The best way is to consider the evidence and see which version it supports.

WHAT DOES THE EVIDENCE SAY?

For time's sake and due to the limited scope of the question, we're not going to look at the evidence for the entire chronology of origins. Let's focus solely on the question at hand regarding dinosaurs.

First, is there any evidence that suggests that dinosaurs and man inhabited the Earth at the same time? YES. There's a strong line of *historical* evidence based on cave drawings and ancient pottery, but our focus in this section is on the extraordinarily strong *scientific* evidence pointing to their coexistence.

We find this evidence in dinosaur fossils. In a relatively recent series of discoveries, dinosaur fossils have given us a wealth of evidence that challenges the naturalist chronology. Let me explain. Numerous scientists examining different dinosaur fossils from multiple excavation sites around the world have found everything from intact cells, skin, ligaments, retinas, blood vessels, etc.[20] Why is this important? Simply because it is impossible that these materials could still be present in bones that have been dead and fossilized for at least sixty-five million years; the soft tissue would have mineralized or decayed long ago. We know this because the biochemistry of molecular decay reveals that these types of materials cannot survive any more than a few thousand years after the death of the animal.

These discoveries scientifically support the position that dinosaurs **did not** die sixty-five million years ago. For the soft tissue to be preserved, these dinosaurs must have died only thousands of years ago. That would place them on Earth at the same time as humans. Imagine that!

For the soft tissue to be preserved, these dinosaurs must have died only thousands of years ago. That would place them on Earth at the same time as humans.

---

[20]Brian Thomas, "Published Reports of Original Soft Tissue Fossils," *Institute for Creation Research* (September 17, 2018). For a long list of soft tissue discovered in dinosaur fossils, go to https://www.icr.org/soft-tissue-list. This list is of those discoveries exclusively published in scientific peer-reviewed journals.

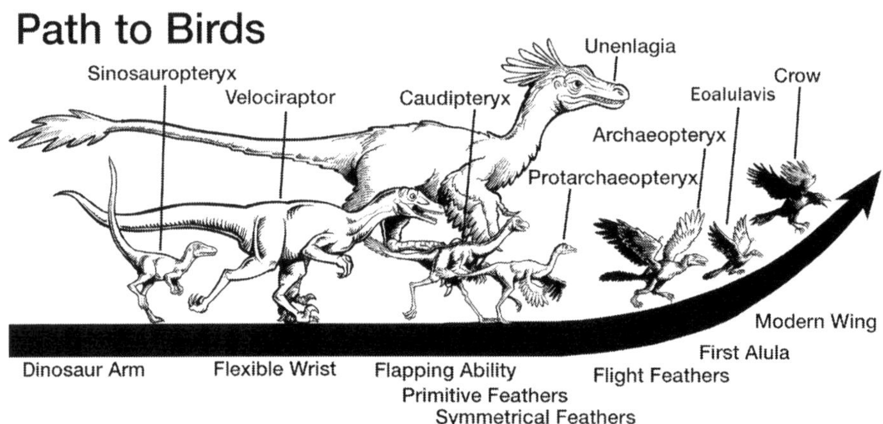

A SELF-STUDY CHALLENGE

Question: Do you know what the scientific evidence does NOT support?

Answer: The claim that over the course of millions of years, naturalistic processes turned dinosaurs into birds.

I will share just one clear example of deception on this topic that many people will never see. This will require some work on your end, but it's worth it, trust me.

- Do a Google IMAGES search for, "Path to Birds." You'll see an image like the one above.[21]
- Then, take the name of each of the examples that you see on the chart and do another Google search.
- Get three secular sources–it doesn't matter which ones you use; you're just not allowed to use any of those "lying" Christian materials.
- Document two simple things:
    1. What was the actual evidence that was found to support the really cool image you see?
    2. How long ago did each of them live according to evolutionist teaching?

I'm not going to tell you the results. I want you to search for yourself because when you've done that, it will mean so much more. I'm confident that you'll see how much is manufactured from how little evidence and that the picture does NOT support what the artist's image

[21]Patterned after an image in *National Geographic*, July 1998: 90-91.

supposedly depicts. I'll tell you up front that the artist's images are a complete and total lie, but you will not know that unless you do the research to find the truth!

Here's a hint: Take special notice of the ages you'll find for the supposed precursor to birds, Velociraptor, and the supposed example of a transitional fossil between dinosaurs and birds, Archaeopteryx. 'Nuff said!

Now let's tie up a loose end: If God created dinosaurs, then why is the word "dinosaur" not found in the Bible? That's quite simple: The word did not exist in biblical times. The word "dinosaur" was invented in 1841. But even though the term "dinosaur" isn't used in the Bible, these creatures are definitely referenced. Dinosaurs are included in the language of Day 6 of creation under the category of "beasts of the earth." In addition, specific references to dinosaurs are found in other places in the Bible, with a clear example being the behemoth mentioned in Job 40:15.

Dinosaurs are included in the language of Day 6 of creation under the category of "beasts of the earth."

CONCLUSION

Up until recently, the idea of man and dinosaur walking the earth together would have sounded ridiculous from a purely naturalistic perspective, since the timelines don't even come close, but the table has flipped. Considering these numerous discoveries from diverse regions of the world, by multiple scientists, with repeatable and consistent test results, it's now much more ridiculous to accept the current naturalistic timeline regarding dinosaurs and modern man. The version we find in God's word is the one that corresponds with reality.

Chapter 10

DID GOD USE EVOLUTION TO CREATE THE WORLD?

Dave Glander

To reconcile the claims of modern "science" with what is recorded in the Bible, it's often been suggested that perhaps God used evolution to create the world, then continued to orchestrate evolution to result in human beings.

This position is problematic on multiple levels, but in this short chapter, we'll only deal with a few of them. First, let's investigate what the evolutionists claim happened, then we'll see if the character and person of God could have used that process to bring about mankind.

BLIND CHANCE – RANDOM – ACCIDENTAL – OR NOT?

To make their claims believable, architects and defenders of the evolutionist worldview lean heavily on two essential concepts, "Natural Selection" and "Beneficial Mutations." Unfortunately for them, both (as *they* define them) are very slippery slopes. Lest I be accused of drawing an inaccurate picture, I will use their own words to define these essential terms.

> **nat·u·ral se·lec·tion: noun**
>
> *The process whereby organisms better adapted to their environment tend to survive and produce more offspring. The theory of its action was first fully expounded by Charles Darwin and is now believed to be the main process that brings about evolution.*[19]

According to the evolutionistic definition then, natural selection chooses from varying mutations within a genome[22] and picks the favorable mutations that will improve the genetic structure of that species. Without a doubt, tiny (but observable) mutations, known as "micro-mutations," occur by the thousands every day. They're so small, however, that they generally have little effect on the genome of the species. However, most evolutionists would also make the claim that genetic mutations occur by *"chance"* or at *"random"* with respect to favorable adaptation. This claim dates to Darwin's conception of *"spontaneous," "accidental,"* or *"chance"* variation.[23] The highly acclaimed *Nature* magazine makes the statement:

> That mutations are random is both profoundly true and profoundly untrue at the same time. The true aspect of this statement stems from the fact that, to the best of our knowledge, the consequences of a mutation have no influence whatsoever on the probability that this mutation will or will not occur. In other words, mutations occur randomly with respect to whether their effects are useful.[24]

So, on the one hand, evolutionists claim that their basic building block, mutations, occur by random, blind chance. As one source states: "This is what we mean by 'evolution is blind.' It cannot anticipate the

---

[22]Oxford Languages/Google Dictionary: The complete set of genetic information in an organism. It provides all the information the organism requires to function.

[23]Charles Darwin, *On the Origin of Species*, 1859, 1868; Charles Darwin and Sir Francis Seward (ed.), *More Letters of Charles Darwin*, 1903.

[24]Laurence Loewe, "Genetic Mutation," *Nature Education* 1(1):113. https://www.nature.com/scitable/ topicpage/genetic-mutation-1127/

future needs of an organism. All it does is adapt a population to its present environment."[25]

On the other hand, while admitting that the process of evolution cannot anticipate future needs and thus direct mutations toward that end, evolutionists teach that Natural Selection is essentially a brain behind the advancement of the genome, "selecting" specific characteristics to include to advance the genome, as well as eventually changing it into a new species (i.e., ape-like creatures developing into modern man). You can't have it both ways! Their slippery slope is that even if Natural Selection as a brain-force advancing the species *could* be true, it would still be forced to choose from blind, unguided, random, and accidental mutations. Logic tells us that blind, accidental processes will not build a thriving, reproducible species. From Charles Darwin's famous book, *The Origin of Species*, we read,

> To sum up, I believe that species come to be tolerably well-defined objects, and do not at any one period present an inextricable chaos of varying and intermediate links: firstly, because new varieties are very slowly formed, for variation is a very slow process, **and natural selection can do nothing until favourable variations chance to occur**[26] (emphasis added).

Richard Dawkins, another proponent of evolution, is the leading advocate for modern evolutionary models as originally prescribed by Charles Darwin. The back cover of his book, *The Blind Watchmaker: Why Evidence of Evolution Reveals a Universe without Design,* reads in part: "In *The Blind Watchmaker,* Richard Dawkins crafts an elegant riposte to show that the complex process of Darwinian natural selection is **unconscious** and automatic. If natural selection can be said to play the role of a watchmaker in nature, it is a **blind one**—working **without foresight** or purpose"[27] (emphasis added). According to modern evolutionary theory, not only are mutations blind and unguided, so is

---

[25]Fallacy Man, "Evolution is Blind," *The Logic of Science*, March 29, 2015. https://thelogicofscience.com/ 2015/03/29/evolution-is-blind/

[26]Darwin, ***Origin of Species***, 84.

[27]Richard Dawkins, *The Blind Watchmaker: Why Evidence of Evolution Reveals a Universe without Design* (New York: Norton & Company, Inc, 1986)

the process of Natural Selection. It appears that any way you look at it, the process of evolutionary theory rests purely on chance alone, without any guarantees for success, and is completely unaided.

WHEN "GOOD" IS NOT GOOD

As mentioned earlier, mutations are observed to happen in the world around us. Most of these mutations are relatively harmless, but some are harmful. A small percentage, though, can be helpful–allowing a species to better adapt to and thrive in their environment. For example, when a species migrates to a colder environment, those animals who have a genetic mutation for thicker coats will weather the change (Pardon the pun!) better than those without that genetic mutation. Maybe a species moves to a new climate that has higher oxygen levels, so those members of the species with stronger lungs suffer less from the thinner air, thus surviving and passing on their genetic strengths (and weaknesses!).

Charles Darwin commented on this reality by saying that, "The case, also, is very interesting, as it proves that with animals, as with plants, any amount of modification in structure can be affected by the accumulation of numerous, slight, and as we must call them accidental, variations, which are … profitable, without exercise or habit having come into play."[28]

All scientists, whether evolutionists or creationists, agree with the basic tenant of mutational adaptation. However, this is where the evolutionist's second slippery slope enters the argument.

ben·e·fi·cial: adjective

Favorable or advantageous; resulting in good[29]

Evolutionists state that Natural Selection chooses only the most beneficial mutations that occur within the genome to pass on to the next generation, thus advancing the overall intelligence of the genome and making an improvement from the previous generation. While some mutations can be considered "beneficial" in that they prove helpful to the species, evolution blatantly disregards another unavoidable and scientifically proven truth: that is, that *ALL mutations come at a cost*

[28]Darwin, *Origin of Species*, 113.

[29]Oxford Languages/Google Dictionary.

to the genome. **Every time a mutation occurs, the genome actually LOSES some of the information it originally started with.**

As a matter of fact, there is no evidence that there's any mechanism that can ADD information to the genetic code while undergoing a mutation. So even though a mutation may have been beneficial to the species, it came at a cost that can never be replaced. In his book, *In the Beginning was Information*, Dr. Werner Gitt (a genetic information specialist) says the following:

> Can new information originate through mutations? This idea is central in representations of evolution, but mutations can only cause changes in existing information. There can be no increase in information, and in general the results are injurious. New blueprints for new functions or new organs cannot arise; mutations cannot be the source of new (creative) information.[30]

Along the same line of thought, former Cornell University geneticist, Professor Dr. J.C. Sanford observes the following:

> However, I believe the "going down" aspect of the genome is subject to actual scientific analysis. It is for this reason that I have focused on the issue of the degradation of information. I believe it is subject to concrete analyses. Such analysis persuasively argues that **net** information must be declining. If this is true, then even if it could be shown that there were specific cases where new information **might** be synthesized via mutation/selection, it would be meaningless–since such new information would promptly then begin to degenerate again. The net direction would still be **down**,

Every time a mutation occurs, the genome actually LOSES some of the information it originally started with.

[30]Werner Gitt, *In the Beginning Was Information* (Green Forest, AR: Master Books, 2006), 127.

> and complex genomes could never have arisen spontaneously. If the genome is actually degenerating, it is bad news for the long-term future of the human race[31] (emphasis in original).

Speaking to Carl Kerby, one of my colleagues, Dr. Sanford said, "Carl, people who tell me that mutation is the process by which information was gained to create a new species are telling me that if I had a 1968 VW Beetle in my driveway, all I'd have to do is go out every day and hit it with a hammer 100 times and I'd get a Porsche 911 in a few million years!" The bottom line is that it just doesn't work.

As we saw earlier, experts in evolutionary theory teach that the process of evolutionary mutation to achieve higher life forms depends on unguided, random, and blind chances. However, all honest scientists realize that mutations actually occur at an extreme cost to the genome and cannot add information. Creationists agree that mutations occur, but God doesn't instigate them … they are a result of living in a fallen, sinful world. Moreover, there is a limit even to adaptation. A land-dwelling creature may adapt to changes in temperature, but it cannot adapt to an all-water environment.

COULD GOD HAVE USED EVOLUTION?

Christian proponents of the teaching that God used the evolutionary process to create the world must be able to answer how the very essence of God's attributes can possibly be reconciled with Darwinian evolution. The Bible makes it clear what God is like and what He is not like. To form an opinion about God's character outside of Scripture is impossible; you can't know who God is without using the Word of God. Without the Bible as your foundation, your opinion is

---

[31] John C. Sanford, *Genetic Entropy & The Mystery Of The Genome* (Longmeadow, MA: FMS Publishing, 2008), Ch.1.

based on a straw man.[32] Let us consider some of God's attributes to see if they are compatible with Him using evolution as a mechanism to create life. Based on what God has revealed about Himself, it is impossible for Him to have used millions of years of death and suffering to create man.

IS THERE ANYTHING GOD CANNOT DO?

The basic question is, can God do anything He wants (i.e., use evolution to create the world if He chose to), or is He limited? Believe it or not, there are some things that God cannot do ***because*** He is God. His very nature as God, revealed to us through the Bible, prohibits Him from telling a lie (Hebrews 6:18) or breaking a promise (Psalm 89:34). God cannot change (Malachi 3:6; Hebrews 13:8) and cannot stop loving you (Jeremiah 31:3; Deuteronomy 7:7-9). God's character, revealed in this way, is a great source of security and comfort for the Christian! Knowing that there are certain things God cannot do because of His character will help us answer whether or not God could have, or would have, used evolution as a means to create the world around us.

GOD DOESN'T DO ANYTHING BY RANDOM, ACCIDENTAL CHANCE!

Throughout Scripture we find numerous passages that explicitly teach God's purposeful design in all that He did. For example, in Isaiah we read, "I am God, and there is no other; I am God, and there is none like me, declaring the end from the beginning and from ancient times things not yet done, saying, 'My counsel shall stand, and I will accomplish all my purpose'" (Isaiah 46:9-10). Even before God spoke creation into existence, He said, "He chose us in him before the foundation of the world, that we should be holy and blameless before him… For we are his workmanship, created in Christ Jesus for good works, which God prepared beforehand, that we should walk in them" (Ephesians 1:2; 2:10). God knows exactly what He is doing at all times and doesn't do anything by random, accidental chance!

---

[32]The straw man fallacy is common in political debates and in discussions over controversial topics. The basic structure of the argument consists of Person A making a claim, Person B creating a distorted version of the claim (the "straw man"), and then Person B attacking this distorted version in order to refute Person A's original assertion. See https://examples.yourdictionary.com/straw-man-fallacy-examples.html

GOD IS THE ULTIMATE GUIDE!

Numerous passages in the Bible teach us of God's guidance for our lives. God made a promise to Jeremiah that can be a hope for all of us, too– "For I know the plans I have for you, declares the LORD, plans for welfare and not for evil, to give you a future and a hope" (Jeremiah 29:11). Proverbs tells us that "The heart of man plans his way, but the LORD establishes his steps" (Proverbs 16:9). King David gave praise to God's leadership when he said, "Through Your precepts I get understanding; therefore, I hate every false way. Your word is a lamp to my feet and a light to my path" (Psalm 119:104-105). These Scriptures clarify for us that God is the true Guide behind His design in creation. His character wouldn't allow Him to use a blind process to direct the creation of the world around us, because He takes personal interest in us.

God knows exactly what He is doing at all times and doesn't do anything by random, accidental chance!

Any attempt to insert the character and essence of God into the evolutionary model quickly reveals that its basic processes are in direct violation to God's character as revealed in the Bible. It's not only the biblical position that God cannot use evolution; it's actually the definitions above used by evolutionists that renders it impossible for Him to do so. For God to have used Darwinian Evolution as His means to create our world, He would be contradicting what He said in His Word, and that's something He *cannot* do.

Bottom line: Could God have created by using evolution? Yes! God could also have created everything in six seconds, in six million years, or by pulling everything out of a hat, but He didn't. He CHOSE to do it the way that He said He did. Otherwise, He would be lying, which He cannot do (Hebrews 6:18).

It is by faith that "we understand that the universe was created by the word of God, so that what is seen was not made out of things that are visible," because, "By the word of the LORD the heavens were made, and by the breath of His mouth all their host … All things were made through Him, and without Him was not anything made that was made… O Lord, how manifold are your works! In wisdom have you made them all; the earth is full of your creatures. Here is the sea, great and wide, which teems with creatures innumerable, living things both small and great," so we "give thanks to you, O God; we give thanks, for your name is near. We recount your wondrous deeds." (Hebrews 11:3; Psalm 33:6; John 1:3; Psalm 104:24-25; Psalm 75:1)

CONCLUSION

There are two basic ways to view the world around us: 1) We can choose to believe that man's words and opinions are the ultimate source of truth, or 2) we can believe that God's Word, the Bible, is the ultimate source of truth. It is through His Word that we know God's character (otherwise we are making guesses about what He is like and what He might have done).

Therefore, the biggest problem with the claim that God might have used evolution to create the universe is that it contradicts the way He said that He did it–by His spoken Word, in six literal days. Any effort made to harmonize man's fluid explanations with God's unchanging Word is an attempt to place man's wisdom on the same level as God's Word. God's Word and His power will always win out in the end (Job 38).

Chapter 11

WERE CAVEMEN AND CAVEWOMEN ANCESTORS TO HUMANS TODAY?[33]

CARL KERBY

My answer may surprise you. Yes and no! How non-committal can you get, right? That'd be like the shortest chapter you've ever read in a book for sure! Sorry, but the explanation isn't quite that short and simple, so let's dig in!

[33]When this question was asked at a camp where I was speaking, I had a good idea of what the questioner was getting at, but I didn't want to assume, so I asked for clarification. Fortunately, the young lady was willing to explain what she meant. She told us that in her high school biology class, the teacher had shared the "evidence" for our supposed human ancestors. In fact, her entire high school experience, plus what is promoted through the media and culture around her, all reinforced the teaching that man arose by a process of small changes over long periods of time, commonly known as "evolution." Those changes took us from ape-like ancestors to more advanced quasi-humans that lived in caves, and eventually evolved into modern-day humans. Her question, as I knew it would be, was directed towards "cavemen" in an evolutionary sense, and specifically, Neanderthal man.

ARE THERE APELIKE ANCESTORS LEADING UP TO MODERN MAN?

I say "No," because the actual scientific evidence doesn't support a supposed common ancestor between apes and humans, which developed into "cavemen," and then eventually turned into today's apes and humans. We find no scientific evidence for this because there **weren't any** evolutionary ancestors preceding apes and humans, and the evidence we discover corroborates that statement! In the fossil record, you'll find apes and you'll find humans. But you won't find anything showing they came from the same source.

Some eager creationist apologists still ask, *"If man evolved from apes, why do we still have apes?"* While this question may get a chuckle or two, the problem with it is that the evolutionary story *no longer* teaches that man evolved from apes. The response of evolutionists has, shall we say, "changed over time." (Hmmmm, there's an example of "real evolution" right there.) Beliefs, words, etc. have changed over time. Humans, on the other hand, have not.

It is true that, in the past, this apes-to-human connection was explicitly taught, and if you dig a little, you will find that it is still being taught today. To verify that, just look at the names of our supposed evolutionary ancestors. Take "Australopithecus" for example … This family includes the most famous of humankind's supposed ancestors, Lucy. Yet this name literally means, "Southern Ape."[34] So, if humans supposedly evolved from this family, as they teach, then according to their evolutionary terminology, we DID evolve from apes! They will still play word games with you, though, if you ask the question like I did above.

To defend my statement that there aren't ANY evolutionary ancestors of apes and humans, allow me to submit "Exhibit A." This is a chart modeled from *Scientific American* (NOT a Christian publication!) depicting this process. Take a look at the chart at right.

Let's explore a brief overview of a few of these supposed evolutionary human ancestors, starting from the very bottom and working our way to the top.

---

[34]Lisa Hendry, *"Australopithecus afarensis,* Lucy's species," *Natural History Museum.* https://www.nhm.ac.uk/discover/australopithecus-afarensis-lucy-species.html

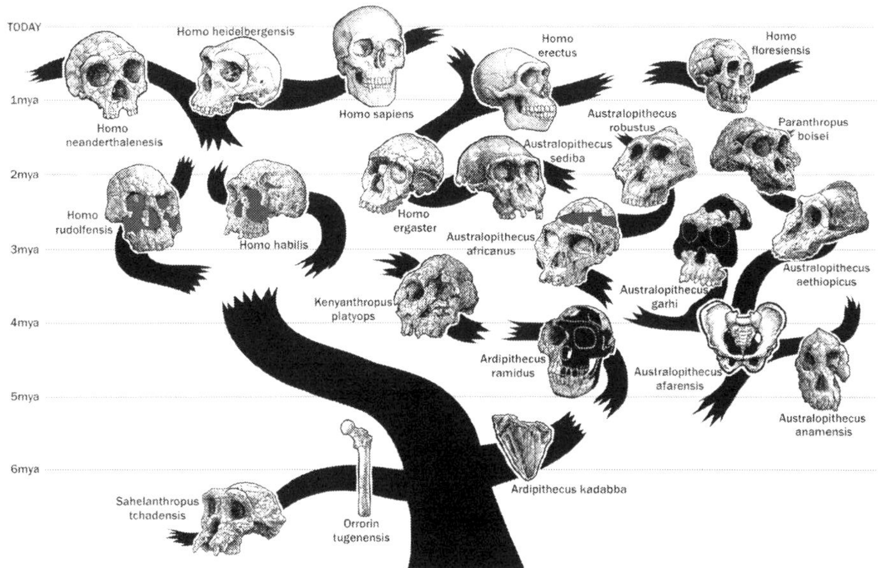

SAHELANTHROPUS TCHADENSIS

(Toumai – Meaning "Hope of Life" in the local Daza language)

What was found? One extremely crushed and distorted skull, and NO bones below the skull. Why is this important? Because without any bones below the skull, it's impossible to know how that specimen actually walked. How do they know Sahelanthropus walked upright, like humans, and not on all fours, like apes? I won't go deep, but the claim is that the "foramen magnum," the hole in the bottom of the skull where the spinal cord exits, proved this.

However, there is debate over the placement of this hole. *Talk Origins*, which is NOT a Christian site, says: "Other scientists have pointed out the foramen magnum (the hole through which the spinal cord exits the skull) of Toumai is positioned towards the back of the skull as in apes, indicating that the skull was held forward and not balanced on top of an erect body."[35]

But, even if it were the same as humans, that still doesn't prove any-

---

[35]Jim Foley," Fossil Hominids FAQs: TM 266-01-060-1 (Toumai)," *Talk Origins*. http://www.talkorigins.org/ faqs /homs/toumai.html

thing. An article in *National Geographic* stated: "A connection between the foramen magnum and bipedalism seems right, but **there's not much hard evidence to back up the link**"[36] (emphasis added).

There's an even bigger problem than that. Look at what is said about where the skull was found: "The remains were not found in the area's fossil deposit, but instead they had weathered out of the 7-million-year-old rock and may have even been moved by people sometime before their discovery."[37]

To be perfectly clear, these scientists admit they have no clue where this extremely "distorted" skull was originally deposited. This means they can't be certain of its age, even according to the evolutionary timespan. If they aren't sure which rock layer it was found in, they can't date it. The facts we know are: It was actually found lying on the dirt and was probably moved there by someone.[38]

What's the Truth About Sahelanthropus?

It's NOT in the human lineage! In 2006, a study by a group of researchers, including Milford Wolpoff of the University of Michigan and John Hawks of the University of Wisconsin, was released suggesting that: *"Sahelanthropus was not a hominid, just some kind of ape."*[39] To drive the point home, look at a quote from Dr. Eugene M. McCarthy, who compared Sahelanthropus to Orrorin (which we'll deal with next). He said: *"...unlike Sahelanthropus tchadensis, which was once billed as the earliest hominid, but now considered a Miocene ape.*"[40] I'd encourage you to read the entire article, which can be found with an internet

---

[36]"The Way You Walk Is Tied to a Hole in Your Skull," *National Geographic*, September 28, 2013. https://www.nationalgeographic.com/science/article/the-way-you-walk-is-tied-to-a-hole-in-your-skull

[37]Brian Switek, "Ancestor Worship," *Wired*, February 22, 2011. https://www.wired.com/2011/02/ ancestor-worship/

[38]Eugene M. McCarthy, "Orrorin tugenensis: The first bipedal hominid?" *Macroevolution.net* (nd). http://www.macroevolution.net/orrorin-tugenensis.html#.U004SuZdU0

[39]Erin Wayman, "Sahelanthropus tchadensis: Ten Years After the Discovery," *Smithsonian Magazine*, July 16, 2012. http://www.smithsonianmag.com/science-nature/sahelanthropus-tchadensis-ten-years-after-the-disocvery-2449553/

[40]McCarthy, "Orrorin tugenensis...," Macroevolution.net (n.d.). http://www.macroevolution.net/orrorin-tugenensis.html#. U004SuZdU0

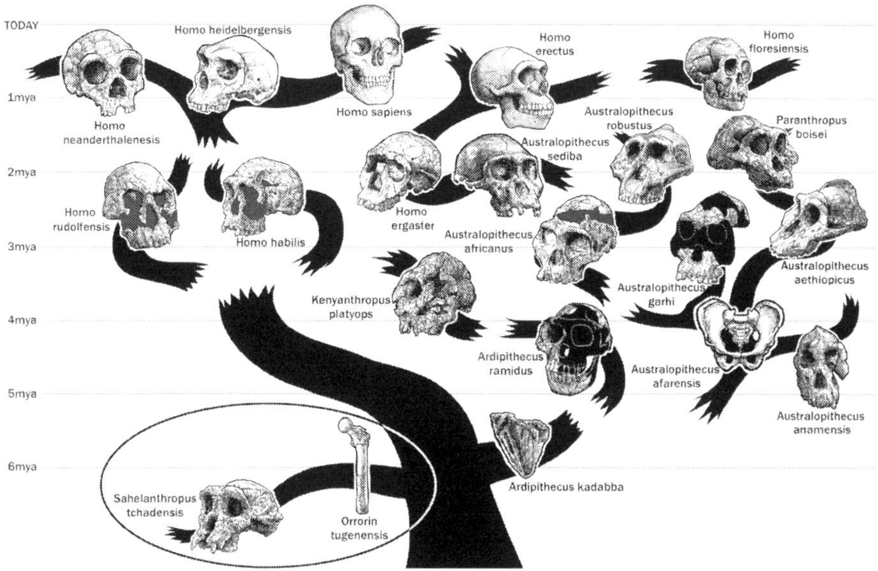

search for "Secret hominin femur still an anthropological mystery."[41] Sahelanthropus is not something we should be worried about!

ORRORIN TUGENESIS
(Meaning "Original Man" in the Tugen language)

What was found? Orrorin is known from about twenty pieces, including a partial femur, some teeth, and a few pieces of the lower jaw.[42] It's said that *"The most important fossil of this species is an upper femur,"*[43] because it supposedly shows evidence that this creature was "bipedal." This simply means that it walked on two legs, as most humans do, instead of walking on all four, being "quadrupedal," which is the predominant mode of locomotion for apes.

What's the Truth About Orrorin?

Let's go to the Australian Museum and see the evidence for Orrorin walking upright and being in the supposed human lineage:

---

[41]Emma Flickinger, "Secret hominin femur still an anthropological mystery," *The Tartan*, January 28, 2018. https://www.pbs.org/wgbh/evolution/humans/humankind/a.html

[42]"Evolution: Origins of Humankind," *PBS* (n.d.). https://www.pbs.org/wgbh/evolution/humans/ humankind/a.html

[43]"What does it mean to be human?" *Smithsonian National Museum of Natural History* (n.d.). https://humanorigins.si.edu/evidence/human-fossils/species/orrorin-tugenensis

"This is contrary to the beliefs of a vast majority of paleoanthropologists and there is not enough evidence to support the argument due to the fragmentary nature of the remains."[44]

With only about twenty pieces of bone, it's next to impossible to prove what this truly was, though evolutionists confidently tout it as an ancestor to humans.

WHAT ABOUT THE REST OF THE ANCESTORS?

The rest of the chart includes LOTS of names … should we be worried? Take a look:

Ardipithecus kadabba Ardipithecus ramidus
Kenyanthropus platyops
Australopithecus africanus
Australopithecus anamensis
Australopithecus garhi Australopithecus sediba
Austrolopithecus robustus
Paranthropus bдise Paranthropus aethiopicus
Australopithecus afarensis

Now that's a massive amount of evidence being provided to prove that over time an ape-like creature turned into man! What can we do?

First, we should NOT give up on God. Concluding that the Bible must be wrong because of all this "evidence" that is being presented would be a mistake, and here's why. For the sake of time, I won't go through what was found for every one of these names, though I challenge you to dig into the topic for yourself. When you do, you'll see that NOT ONE of those names above are in the human lineage. NOT ONE! You can verify that with nothing but secular sources as well. To prove my point quickly, just look at the image again from earlier in this chapter.

Notice their placement on the "tree." Every one of them is off to

---

[44]Fran Dorey, "Orrorin tugenensis," *Australian Museum* (Updated December 19, 2019). https://australian.museum/learn/science/human-evolution/orrorin-tugenensis/#

the right, out of the line to humans at the top! Again, none of them are in the human lineage!

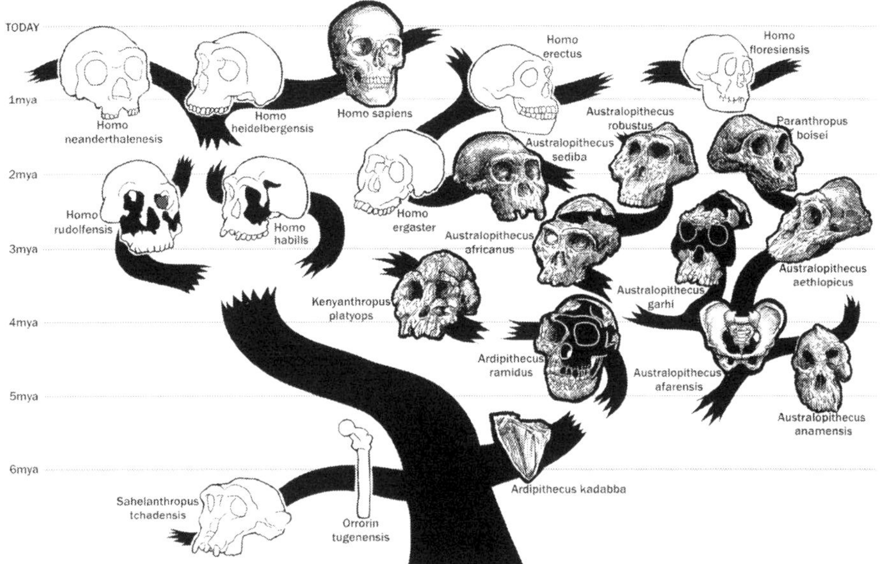

I teach a class on these supposed ancestors and deal with each one individually, again working only from secular sources. But let's just cut to the chase. A tree cannot grow if it doesn't have a trunk or roots! By de-bunking the trunk and roots of this supposed evolutionary tree, the entire tree's worth as "evidence" is shown to be barren and desolate.

That's why I said "no" to the original question of "Were cavemen and cavewomen human ancestors?" But if you remember, I also answered "Yes." Why so? The answer is simple. The original question referred specifically to Neanderthal man, so let's deal with that one.

It's important in dealing with this, as well as any other controversial issue, to realize that both evolutionists and creationists have the same evidence. In this case, there's solid evidence showing that caves were used as lodging for human beings. In fact, the Bible itself has quite a few verses talking about men that lived in caves. David lived in the cave of Adullam for a while.[45] Job 30:6 speaks of those who lived in "holes of the earth and of the rocks," while Hebrews 11:38 mentions those who lived "in dens and caves of the earth."

---

[45]Read 1 Samuel 22:1; 2 Samuel, 23:13; and 1 Chronicles 11:15.

CONCLUSION

Even secular scientists will admit that Neanderthal interbred with modern-day humans.[46] You can even take a genetic test to see if you have Neanderthal DNA or not. If you have red hair, there is a higher chance you have some Neanderthal in your lineage.[47] Neanderthal lived in caves,[48] buried their dead,[49] and in fact have been found in these graves alongside modern-day humans.[50] They also wore jewelry,[51] made tools,[52] and created art.[53]

So, biblically speaking, the Neanderthals were humans with unique and specific physical traits that probably lived just after the flood. As humankind multiplied and spread over the face of the Earth, it would have been simpler and smarter to move into caves (when they were available) than to build housing. Evolutionists must deal with this same evidence for cave-dwellers, but their explanation is far different from the biblical one. That's NOT because of the evidence; it's because of their worldview. Dr. Joe Cain, of University College London, makes it very easy to understand what Neanderthals were. He said: "Neanderthal at best is a man with some ape qualities."[54]

So, yes, there were "cavemen!" They were nothing more than humans with some unique physical characteristics that lived in caves. That is the truth, and that is what the evidence supports!

---

[46]Michael D. Gregory, M.D., J. Shane Kippenhan, Daniel P. Eisenberg, et al. "Neanderthal-Derived Genetic Variation Shapes Modern Human Cranium and Brain," *Sci Rep* 7, 6308 (2017). https://doi.org/10.1038/s41598-017-06587-0

[47]Melissa Hogenboom. "What did the Neanderthals do for us?" *BBC Earth*, November 16, 2015.

[48]Melissa Hogenboom. "How did the last Neanderthals live?" *BBC Future*, January 29, 2020. https://www.bbc.com/ future/article/20200128-how-did-the-last-neanderthals-live

[49]Richard G. Klein. ***The Human Career: Human Biological and Cultural Origins*** (Chicago: The University of Chicago Press, 1989), 236-237.

[50]Robert S. Corruccini. "Metrical Reconsideration of the Skull IV and IX and Border Cave 1 Crania in the Context of Modern Human Origins," *American Journal of Physical Anthropology* 87:4 (April 1992): 433-445.

[51]Juan Luis De Arsuaga. *The Neanderthal's Necklace: In Search of the First Thinkers* (Hoboken, NJ: Wiley, 2003), 192.

[52]Kate Wong, "Neanderthal Notes," *Scientific American* (September 1997), 28-30; "Early Music," *Science* 276, April 11, 1997: 205.

[53]Klein, *The Human Career,* 440.

[54]"Ape to Man," *The History Channel* (June 13, 2014), 13:44. https://www.youtube.com/ watch?v= 4K8MeFQp7u4

Chapter 12

IS THE EARTH 415 MILLION YEARS OLD?

JUAN VALDES

This question reveals that rabbits aren't the only things that can magically be pulled out of thin air ... the age of the Earth can also be randomly selected at will. Apparently, 415 million years is a purely random number, chosen perhaps as the biggest the questioner could contrive.

Dwarfing this number, the current cosmological model dates the world at more than *four billion* (not million) years old. In comparison, the biblical model dates it in the thousands of years old, not millions or billions. However, the question behind the question is what really matters: How old *is* the Earth?

We at Reasons for Hope believe Earth is a young planet in a young universe. Thus, what follows are some of the main biblical and scientific arguments in support of that idea.

THE CASE FOR A YOUNG EARTH

The Bible does not give a specific date for creation, nor are there verses stating the specific age of the universe or the age of the Earth. However, there are contextual clues in the Bible that stand in strong defense of a young Earth.

One of the strongest biblical arguments for a young Earth comes from a careful analysis of the genealogies found in Genesis. This is known as the **Argument from Genealogies.** It is widely agreed that Jesus lived ~2,000 years ago and that Abraham lived ~2,000 years before Jesus. The Argument from Genealogies says that, based on the generations listed in Genesis 5 and 11, Adam lived ~2,000 years before Abraham. Some dispute whether these genealogies are "closed" or "open." The difference between the two is that a closed genealogy has no gaps; the chronology provided covers the time specified without skipping any generations. Open genealogies are those that have gaps in between the generations listed. The argument is that if the genealogies are open, the missing portions could extend the age of the Earth, justifying an old Earth perspective.

However, the overlap between each of the generations presented renders meaningless any possible gaps. For example, Adam was 130 years old when he had Seth, and Adam continued living for 800 more years. Seth also lived those 800 years overlapping with his dad, plus 112 additional years. Seth's son, Enosh, overlapped with his dad 807 years. It's easy to track these overlaps from person to person all the way to Abraham, with the conclusion that there were ~2,000 years between Adam and Abraham, regardless of any possible gaps. So, it is reasonable to say that man has been on this Earth for approximately 6,000 years.

A simple reading of Genesis 1-2 leaves no room for any evolutionary processes leading up to mankind.

Some object to the genealogies by arguing that Adam was not necessarily the first man. This is a common position among theistic evolutionists who believe that Adam was the product of millions of years of evolution. However, God's Word is clear about Adam being the first human. A simple reading of Genesis 1-2 leaves no room for any evolutionary processes leading up to mankind. In addition, Jesus Himself spoke of Adam as the first man (Mark 10:6-8), as did Paul (1 Corinthians 15:45,47; Romans 5:12-14; 1 Timothy 2:13).

Another common objection to the genealogies attempts to bypass them altogether by arguing that the age of the Earth does not begin with Adam in Genesis 1:26, but rather with Genesis 1:1. The idea being presented is that the days of creation were long periods of time, ranging from several thousand to millions of years (depending on whose model you look at). With this view, by the time Adam shows up, the Earth could potentially already be millions or maybe billions of years old. However, this position is impossible to hold if one is to be faithful to the text of the Bible.

To begin with, I challenge you to find ten people (or 50 or 1000) and have them read Genesis 1-2. Ask them what the plain reading of the text says. I predict that 100% of the participants will admit that the text clearly speaks of God creating everything in six ordinary days and resting on the seventh. It seems obvious that NOTHING in those two chapters gives any hint of the days being symbolic, allegorical, figurative, poetic, etc. In fact, applying proper exegesis (biblical interpretation) to the passages shows how God went out of His way to emphasize and re-emphasize that they were literal days. It wasn't sufficient to use the Hebrew word for day (*yom*, יוֹם) by itself, since the word *yom* can be correctly interpreted in different ways according to the context—not just as literal 24-hour days. God seemed to go out of His way to eliminate any possible ambiguity by modifying that noun with *two* sets of modifiers.

When speaking of the days of creation, the noun *yom* is modified with a number (e.g., "the first day" in Gen. 1:5). Nearly every time *yom* appears with a number in the rest of the Bible, it means a literal day. There are only two exceptions to this rule (Zechariah 14:7; Hosea 6:2), but the context of those passages clearly indicates that they are speaking prophetically about the coming Day of the Lord. But just to make sure we didn't misunderstand, God added another layer of modifiers that are only understood in the context of literal days. When speaking of the days of creation, the word *yom* is always modified with the phrase "and there was evening and there was morning." Again, every time the word *yom* is accompanied by the word "evening" and/or "morning" in the rest of the Bible, it is understood as a literal day. Take a closer look at the emphasis:

- And there was **evening** and there was **morning,** the **first** day. (1:5)
- And there was **evening** and there was **morning,** the **second** day. (1:8)
- And there was **evening** and there was **morning,** the **third** day. (1:13)
- And there was **evening** and there was **morning,** the **fourth** day. (1:19)
- And there was **evening** and there was **morning,** the **fifth** day. (1:23)
- And there was **evening** and there was **morning,** the **sixth** day. (1:31)

Any interpretation of these days as anything other than literal days violates the expressed intent of the author of the text. Not to mention that in the Ten Commandments (written by God Himself using His finger on clay tablets), God told us that He created the world and everything in it in six days before resting the seventh day (Exodus 20:11).[55]

Other attempts to insert millions or billions into the history of creation have also failed, but the most common are the Gap Theory, the Prior Creation Theory, and the Framework Hypothesis. Besides the fact that all these theories lack biblical support and are not the result of a plain reading of Genesis, they are plagued with insurmountable difficulties (some of which are dealt with in the next section).

In addition to the Argument from Genealogies, there are scientific arguments that also point towards a young Earth. Let's consider three specific scientific arguments in favor of a young Earth.[56] These are the arguments from entropy, from geology, and from archaeology.[57] Here is a brief summary of each.

---

[55]For more information on this topic, reference the chapter on "Were the days in Genesis actual days?"

[56]Andrew Snelling, *Earth's Catastrophic Past: Geology, Creation & The Flood,* Volumes 1 & 2, (Green Forest, AR: Master Books, 2014).

[57]John C Sanford, *Genetic Entropy* (Longmeadow, MA: FMS Publishing, 2014).

1) Argument from Entropy (a gradual decline into disorder). These arguments from entropy provide evidence that our solar system is suffering a significant decline. It is running out of usable energy (as per the Second Law of Thermodynamics). This decay seems to be pervasive. For example, Earth's magnetic field is decaying at a constant rate. Given this rate of decay, Earth cannot even be millions of years old, and certainly not over *four billion*. By the way, this decay rate isn't only true for Earth, but also all planets in our solar system.

Besides magnetic fields decaying, planetary heat emissions from Jupiter and Neptune are also decaying. These planets have a limited amount of internal heat, yet Jupiter is believed to emit *twice* as much heat as it receives from the sun. Neptune is an even better example, emitting almost *three* times the heat it receives from the sun. Given the amount of heat these planets still have, we know they must be young planets, not even close to millions or billions of years, or they would have no internal heat left.

Much closer to home we have another example of entropy—genetic entropy. Geneticists have repeatedly shown that our genes are decaying consistently from one generation to the next. While it's admittedly difficult to measure the rate of increase of significant genetic defects from one generation to the next, Dr. John C. Sanford, former Cornell University geneticist, estimates that there are approximately one hundred *new* significant mutations in each succeeding generation. This genetic decay rate of the human genome can't support millions of years of evolution because we would have gone extinct several times over by now.

2) Argument from Geology. The Earth's geological features provide additional evidence in support of a young Earth. For example, ocean salinity is constantly increasing at a known rate. Salt is deposited into the oceans via rivers and is removed primarily by evaporation. However, much more is deposited than evaporated. Using current rates, the Earth could not be millions of years old, or the oceans would have reached salt levels so high that life would be impossible. Additional problems arise with the erosion of continents, the sediments in the ocean, levels of helium in the atmosphere, etc.

3) Argument from Human History. Historians agree that written language first appeared some 5,500 years ago. Interestingly, that fits the model of a young Earth quite well. If the Earth was as ancient as evolutionists claim, modern man would have existed for nearly 250,000 years before ever developing a written language. Strains your common sense a bit, doesn't it?

Historians also agree that organized agricultural communities sprung up approximately 10,000 years ago. Again, the facts fit the young Earth model much better than the old Earth model. According to the model of evolution, we are expected to believe that it took modern man almost 250,000 years to figure out how to farm!

And when did the building of large permanent settlements begin? The consensus among historians is that man began to settle in primitive permanent settlements (i.e., towns) around 7,000 years ago. Are you starting to get the picture? The historical evidence easily coincides with the timeframe given using biblical genealogies.

A BIGGER PROBLEM

In addition to the problems already considered above, there is one biblical problem that seems insurmountable to me. If the Earth is billions of years old and man is the product of evolution, then Adam and Eve were preceded by millions of years of ancestors who lived *and died.* Death was a part of our universe long before Adam and Eve sinned. Think about that. Consider God's words directed at Adam and Eve: "And the Lord God commanded the man, saying, 'You may surely eat of every tree of the garden, but of the tree of the knowledge of good and evil you shall not eat, for in the day that you eat of it you shall surely die'" (Genesis 2:16-17).

The clear message is that death was not a part of the world God created until man sinned, disobeying God. That is also what Paul understood when he said, "Therefore, just as sin came into the world through one man, and death through sin, and so death spread to all men because all sinned" (Romans 5:12).

To say that death was a part of this world before Adam's sin is to contradict the clear teaching of the Word of God. In addition, why would God call His creation "GOOD" six times during the creation week and end Day 6 by declaring all that He had done to be "VERY

GOOD"? How could millions of years of illness, birth defects, genetic mutations, decay, and death be very good? For the advocate of an old Earth, this problem of death before Adam's sin is inescapable.

CONCLUSION

How old is the Earth? We do not have a precise number, but considering the biblical narrative of origins, it is reasonable to say that the Earth is anywhere from 6,000-10,000 years old. Unfortunately, this is a minority view, even among Christians, although truth has never been determined by majority. The primary arguments raised against a young Earth stem from valuing the current scientific models above the revelation of God's Word.

For the advocate of an old Earth, this problem of death before Adam's sin is inescapable.

Don't get me wrong: I love science and encourage Christian young people to pursue science. However, we must understand its limits. Science is ever-changing; thus, it doesn't seem wise to take the side of "science" whenever it opposes God's clear revelation. What science affirms as absolute truth today may be discarded tomorrow, as the history of science has shown over and over again. The Word of God is a much firmer foundation to build our model of origins on—since the Word of God doesn't have an expiration date, and it doesn't change with time. As Jesus Himself proclaimed,

Matthew 24:35

Heaven and earth will one day pass away,
but the Word of God will still be standing.

PART THREE

CHRISTIANITY

Chapter 13

HOW DO YOU BRING UP GOD WITH YOUR FRIENDS?

JUAN VALDES

"You're not supposed to talk about politics and religion in polite company!"

Common wisdom, whatever that means, seems to dictate that speaking of such topics inevitably leads to conflict. There seems to be some truth to that, as anyone who's ever been "unfriended" on social media knows. I'm not sure when it happened, but somewhere along the way we lost the ability to disagree amicably with others. Thus, this concept seems to stem from a deep-seated desire to avoid conflict at all costs.

But is it a good idea to always avoid conflict? Is it a good idea to abstain from speaking of certain topics because of the controversy it may provoke? Well, it depends on what the conflict is about. If conflict arises from unimportant and insignificant conversations such as your favorite ice cream or who's the best forward in the NBA, then avoiding said conflict is probably a good idea. However, politics and religion are ***not*** unimportant and insignificant topics. Quite the contrary. Few topics are more significant to mankind than the government that rules over him and his beliefs about God and the ultimate nature of our relationship to Him (i.e., religion).

As we tackle this question, let's break it down into three major issues. First, is it really that important to talk about God or religion? Second, do we have a moral responsibility to engage our friends on these topics? Finally, how should we go about engaging our friends on the topic of God?

IS IT IMPORTANT TO TALK ABOUT GOD AND RELIGION?

Yes! In fact, it is THE most important topic we can ever talk about. The importance stems from the **eternal** implications attached to our beliefs regarding God and the ultimate nature of our relationship to Him. Every other topic we choose to talk about is bound to the temporal world (i.e., the material world, not spiritual). Discussions about diets, heroes, economics, romances, dreams, etc., never have more than temporary implications. At death, the importance of every other conversation dissipates. It is the conversations that lead to our belief or disbelief in God that impact us beyond our earthly existence, and therein lies the importance of this topic.

Everyone has an opinion about God, and that is why there are so many religions in the world. Even atheists have an opinion about God—they believe He does not exist. How do you know, without a doubt, if your opinion about God is true or not if you don't engage with others in discussion? Engaging with others about this allows us not only to examine our position, but also to test our beliefs in the market of ideas. How can someone with the wrong idea ever come to realize it without healthy dialogue about God and the nature of our relationship with Him?

Jesus (i.e., God) asked the disciples in Matthew 16:13, "Who do people say the Son of Man is?" Think of the implications of that question for a second. To answer it, they had to be engaged with the lost! That means WE must be engaged with the lost! Therefore, we ought not avoid conversations about God and religion simply because we wish to avoid conflict.

DO WE HAVE A MORAL OBLIGATION TO ENGAGE OUR FRIENDS ON THESE TOPICS?

Yes! Let's expand on that question a little. Imagine this scenario with me: You're driving across a beautiful mountain range, crossing breathtaking bridges, and enjoying the wonderful scenery when, just as you come out of a hairpin turn, you must slam on the brakes because the bridge ahead has collapsed. Whew! That was close. Now imagine you begin to back your way out of there and notice a friend who is also driving down that road at a high rate of speed. What do you do? Here are your three options:

1) Don't say anything; after all, it's not your problem— you're safe.

2) Don't say anything because it may provoke a conflict with your friend.

3) Do everything you can to stop your friend from driving over the cliff.

If you choose options 1 or 2, unfriend me now! I do not want friends like that. Seriously, though, it's obvious that there's only one thing you are morally obligated to do: The last option—do everything you can to save your friend's life.

Dying is not the worst thing that can happen. Dying without trusting in Jesus for salvation IS the worst thing that can ever happen. It means being ETERNALLY separated from God—it means missing Heaven and spending eternity in Hell. Wouldn't you agree that not engaging our friends on the topic of God and the nature of our relationship with Him is **infinitely worse** than not attempting to warn our friend that the bridge is out?

Dying without trusting in Jesus for salvation IS the worst thing that can ever happen.

Let me tell you what Atheist (and I do mean Atheist with a capital "A"!) Penn Jillette said: "If you believe that there's a Heaven and Hell, and people could be going to Hell or not, getting eternal life or whatever ... How much do you have to hate somebody to not proselytize? How much do you have to hate somebody to believe that everlasting life is possible, and not tell them that?"

As Christians, we *know* the Truth. We know that there's only one way to get to Heaven—trusting Jesus as our Savior. Furthermore, God has made it clear that we must engage with those that have yet to trust Jesus. The great commission is clear. Jesus commands us in both Matthew (28:19,20) and Mark (16:15) to **GO** and share the good news. It's not optional—there's too much at stake. But how can we engage our friends effectively?

HOW SHOULD WE ENGAGE OUR FRIENDS ON THE TOPIC OF GOD?

There are many ways of engaging our friends on the topic of God and the importance of having a relationship with Him through Jesus.[58] One of the strategies that's proven to be highly effective in today's culture is using everyday conversations as a bridge to connect to spiritual topics. This method is effective, in part because the conversation can flow into spiritual topics naturally–like the ones mentioned below–without being forced.

- For example, a wonderful opportunity is presented when your friends ask the ever-popular question, *"How was your weekend?"*
    - You can share something about your weekend, but the highlight or focus of your response should be about your time with God and other believers in a small group or church, and/or your time in God's Word.
    - You could share specifically about the sermon you heard or something you learned from Scripture or something that someone said in your group.
    - You could share a point that was made or how you were personally challenged by what you heard or read. Be authentic!
    - A good follow-up question after you have shared about

[58]We have a wonderful booklet titled, "7 THINGS THAT WILL HELP YOU SHARE YOUR FAITH WITHOUT FEELING LIKE A GOOF" that will help you share your faith successfully. (*Go to https://www.rforh.com/7-things-that-will-help-you-share your-faith to download the free PDF.*)

what you learned or what challenged you is, "What do you think about that?" Then listen. Don't try to plan out what you are going to say next while they're talking. By listening well, you should be able to identify various ways to continue the conversation.

- In the same manner, sports conversations can be turned around to focus on a given athlete or coach that is a committed Christian and how you find that so encouraging.
- People also like to talk about their problems. When they've finished sharing, at a minimum, you can offer to pray for them and their situation. Don't be deceived into thinking that praying for someone or even offering to pray for them isn't going to have an impact. God's Word indicates prayer is powerful (James 5:16). God may also give you words of encouragement to share.

One final suggestion. Sometimes we have opportunities to engage with people who are not necessarily close friends. If you don't have a close relationship with someone, start a conversation with a question like, "What's your story?" or "Tell me about your tattoo!" Yes, tattoos have started some amazing conversations! Typically, there's meaning behind the ink. These are powerful questions that you can ask someone to start building a relationship with them.

Our job is to share the truth with them in love—to give an answer for the hope that lies within us (1 Peter 3:15).

People are often eager to share something about themselves when asked. As people share their stories, there's usually a topic or two that comes up that we can use to connect to God–how He's with us in our most difficult times; how He's that loving father we may have never had; or how He cares about justice and will remedy the wrongs/abuses we've suffered, etc. Furthermore, these types of conversations help us build closer connections with the people we engage. We can be far more effective witnesses to those with whom we have developed a relationship.

CONCLUSION

When someone asks how they can engage their friends on the topic of God, it's a good sign. It means we're worried about our friends' salvation. Don't let yourself be persuaded by the dumb idea that we should never engage in conversations about God. Nothing could be further from the truth. However, it's also important to keep in mind that it's not our job to convert people. ***Our job is to share the truth with them in love***—to give an answer for the hope that lies within us (1 Peter 3:15). Conversion is the job of the Holy Spirit (John 16:7-14). Finally, do not expect to "close the deal" in every conversation you have about God. It often takes a long time for people to shift their worldviews to such a degree where Jesus is what they desire. Sometimes we *are* rewarded with leading a person to a saving faith in Jesus. When that does happen, it's usually because other believers have come before us and planted seeds of truth.

Chapter 14

IS IT POSSIBLE THAT HITLER GOT SAVED RIGHT BEFORE HE DIED? THAT JUST DOESN'T SEEM FAIR.

FRANK FIGUEROA

Before answering this question, we must define what is meant by "fair." The word "fair" (used in this way) means: "Just. Equitable. Impartial. Free from self-interest, prejudice, or favoritism."[59] Another issue we must address is who defines fairness–God or us? In this case, as we'll see, we can be grateful that the authority on this issue rests solely on the heavenly Father's shoulders.

WHAT ARE WE SAVED FROM?

When we look at the question of salvation, we must ask ourselves, "What are we saved from?" I would argue the ultimate answer is what we're all thinking of: Hell, which is eternal destruction and separation from God. We can all imagine the horror of this place and the pain and suffering that will occur there because the Bible is quite explicit in its

[59]Merriam-webster.com

description. In many passages of Scripture, Hell is clearly described as a place of torment. The Bible uses words like weeping (Matthew 8:12); wailing (Matthew 13:42); gnashing of teeth (Matthew 13:50); darkness (Matthew 25:30); flames (Luke 16:24); and everlasting punishment (Luke 16:23) to describe Hell. This is NOT a good place!

Who would knowingly want to go there? The obvious answer is, "No one!" But the tragic reality is that most who end up in Hell will be shocked to find themselves there. Notice the warning that Jesus gives to those who choose to follow Him in Luke 13:24-28:

> Strive to enter through the narrow door. For many, I tell you, will seek to enter and will not be able. When once the master of the house has risen and shut the door, and you begin to stand outside and to knock at the door, saying, "Lord, open to us," then he will answer you, "I do not know where you come from." Then you will begin to say, "We ate and drank in your presence, and you taught in our streets." But he will say, "I tell you; I do not know where you come from. Depart from me, all you workers of evil!" In that place there will be weeping and gnashing of teeth when you see Abraham and Isaac and Jacob and all the prophets in the kingdom of God but you yourselves cast out.

FAIRNESS IS IN THE EYE OF THE BEHOLDER

No one WANTS to go to Hell, but since our question deals with fairness, it might be better to ask, "Who **deserves** to go to a place like this?" We could all have a list as to who deserves Hell, but our answers are usually subjective. It depends on the opinion of the one making the judgment: What sin has been committed? Is it worth ultimate punishment in their eyes? However, when we look at who God says these Hell-bound people are, a terrifying chill should go up our spines.

Since God is the One who created Hell, we would have to concede that He is ultimately the sole judge of who goes there and who doesn't. The terrifying reality is: We all deserve it. God's Word teaches that we have all sinned and fall short of the glory of God (Romans 3:23). It also establishes that the consequence of sin is death (Romans 6:23). This teaching is consistent even in the Old Testament where we read in Ezekiel 18:20, "The soul who sins shall die." This means that the people doomed for destruction include **you and me**! We're all deserving of hellfire and eternal judgment.

In the most loving, merciful, and ultimately "unfair" act anyone has ever done, God sent His Son, Jesus, who willingly came to the Earth and lived the perfect life we couldn't live, died a death we should have died, and paid our sin penalty in full (Ephesians 2:1-10; Romans 5:6-11).

Some would argue that God is the most "unfair" Person ever! Why? Because of His mercy, He didn't give us what we deserved *(Hell and judgment).* Instead, because of His grace, He gave us what we didn't deserve *(everlasting life and adoption into His family).* Let's look at three examples of people who deserved something different than what they received.

MONEY CANNOT BUY OUR SALVATION

A beggar named Lazarus shows us this. We read about him in Luke 16:19-26:

> There was a rich man who was clothed in purple and fine linen and who feasted sumptuously every day. And at his gate was laid a poor man named Lazarus, covered with sores, who desired to be fed with what fell from the rich man's table. Moreover, even the dogs came and licked his sores. The poor man died and was carried by the angels to Abraham's side. The rich man also died and was buried, and in Hades, being in torment, he lifted up his eyes and saw Abraham far off and Lazarus at his side. And he called out, "Father Abraham, have mercy on me, and send Lazarus to dip the end of his finger in water and cool my tongue, for I am in anguish in this flame." But Abraham said, "Child, remember that you in your lifetime received your good things, and Lazarus in like manner bad things; but now he is comforted here, and you are in anguish. And besides all this, between us and you a great chasm has been fixed, in order that those who would pass from here to you may not be able, and none may cross from there to us.

Gallup polls consistently show that most Americans believe in Heaven.[60] Interestingly, it's not uncommon in the polls to find that most people who believe in Heaven think they are going there after they die.

Here's the scary part–so did the rich man in this biblical account! From this account, we discover three certainties that Jesus wants each of us to know:

1) Living is certain.

2) Death is certain.

3) Life after death is certain.

Notice that no matter how much we hear that *paying taxes* is the third thing that's certain in this world, that's NOT what God said. Life after death IS CERTAIN! And where we're going to spend eternity is solely dependent on our relationship with Jesus Christ!

Jesus, THE Life, died so that we who are spiritually dead might have life. This same salvation is offered to every single person, whether it be someone who is morally good in our eyes or someone whose life was as atrocious as Adolf Hitler's. After all, salvation is a gift, not a reward.

The rich man had money. He was dressed in clothes dyed with purple Tyrian dye and lived his life to the hilt. As for the poor man, not only did he not have any money, but what he did have was equally bad … he was covered with ulcerous sores which made him a friend only to the street dogs. But then one day, as Jesus stated, both died. Remember, death is certain.

We have no idea what the rich man's name was or what it meant. But we do know Lazarus' name, which is a Greek translation of the common Hebrew name, Eleazar, meaning, "God is my help." And that's all that matters. We're all like Lazarus … poor, infected, and undeserving. But then Jesus comes along and rescues us, and He knows our name! Praise God for that!

---

[60] "Religion," *Gallup* (n.d.). https://news.gallup.com/poll/1690/religion.aspxl

RELIGION DOESN'T EQUAL SALVATION

Some argue that if we are sincere about our religion, that means we will go to Heaven. But to counter that, all we must do is read the account of Saul of Tarsus (Galatians 1:11-24). As the second-most respected Jew in all of Israel, preceded only by Gamaliel (Acts 22:3-5), Saul was passionately committed to opposing anyone who was against legalistic Judaism, including Christians (Acts 8:1-3; Acts 9:1-2). But God, in His mercy, dramatically revealed Himself to Saul (Acts 22:6-9). At that very moment, his life was radically changed! So much so, that God was going to use Saul, later called Paul, as the man through whom all non-Jews would be reached with the Gospel!

SALVATION IS OFFERED TO THE WORST OF US

The most glaring example of a sinner being offered undeserved salvation is probably the thief who was crucified on the cross next to Jesus (Luke 23:39-43). There were two thieves crucified on the same day as Jesus, and both deserved death. For that matter, they deserved Hell itself. Being criminals, it's no wonder we read in Matthew's account that both were initially mocking Jesus (Matthew 27:44).

While hanging on the cross, others mocked Jesus for not saving Himself and punishing all the sinners responsible for His crucifixion. But, if He had "saved Himself," He wouldn't have been able to save others, including the thief that was now crying out for mercy!

Simply, Heaven is for anyone who trusts that Jesus is the one who has paid the price of their sin, and who lives in repentance and relationship with Him.

Jesus, THE Life, died so that we who are spiritually dead might have life. This same salvation is offered to every single person, whether it be someone who is morally good in our eyes or someone whose life was as atrocious as Adolf Hitler's. After all, salvation is a gift, not a reward.

Notice what Jesus tells the thief: "Assuredly, I say to you, today you will be with Me in Paradise" (Luke 23:43, NKJV). Jesus prefaced His response to the thief with the word, "**assuredly,**" because what He was going to say was going to be hard to believe. The "religious and righteous" people didn't think this thieving sinner was deserving of heaven, but not only was he going there, he was going to be right alongside Jesus as he went!

CONCLUSION

Thank God for His grace!

We should be grateful that instead of giving us what is "fair," God offers us mercy and grace. With these examples, we see clearly that it was possible for Hitler to be saved IF he believed in the Lord Jesus Christ as Scripture states, though it is highly unlikely that he did. The truth is, not all "bad" people go to Hell, nor do all "good" people go to Heaven. Simply, Heaven is for anyone who trusts that Jesus is the one who has paid the price of their sin, and who lives in repentance and relationship with Him.

Chapter 15

WHAT ABOUT PEOPLE WHO DIED BEFORE JESUS SHOWED UP? ARE THEY IN HELL? WHAT HAPPENS TO BABIES WHEN THEY DIE? ARE THEY GOING TO HELL BECAUSE THEY DID NOT ACCEPT JESUS?

JUAN VALDES

Underneath these questions is the broader concern of: "What does perfect justice look like?" From the vantage point of a fallen world, where justice is ever-so-elusive, this question is very difficult to answer. From God's perspective, however, it becomes straightforward. After all, God is perfectly just, therefore His concept of justice is, by definition, a *perfect* concept of justice.

Perfect justice means God ALWAYS does the right thing. From God's perspective, this also means that every sin must be punished, and every single transgression must be dealt with. With God, there is no "sweeping things under the rug." God is incapable of looking the other way and allowing any transgression to go unpunished.

This is NOT good news for us. God says in His word that ALL have sinned and thus, ALL have fallen short of Heaven (Romans 3:23). If everyone ended up in Hell, that would still be perfect justice because we have all earned our spot there via our sins. Thankfully, there is more to God than perfect justice. God is also perfectly loving, perfectly merciful, and perfectly gracious. Because God loves mankind—His special creation—He desires that no one pay the ultimate price for their sin. (Romans 6:23 tells us this price is *death*.) However, He can't just overlook our transgressions. Perfect justice demands that the price of sin (i.e., death) must be paid.

Thankfully, there is more to God than perfect justice. God is also perfectly loving, perfectly merciful, and perfectly gracious.

Even though we are undeserving, God, motivated by His **perfect love**, provided the payment for *every* transgression that has *ever* been committed by man by giving His one and only Son to die at Calvary on our behalf (Romans 5:8; John 3:16). This results in **perfect mercy**. We don't have to get what we deserve; God is able to pardon us through the sacrifice of Christ on the cross. God's **perfect grace** allows us to be given what we don't deserve—forgiveness of our sins and the promise of eternal life. Nevertheless, man still has a choice as to whether he wants to pay his own sin debt or accept Christ's payment on his behalf. *This breathtaking plan is unique to the Christian faith.*

When we review the questions we began with, we see that they seem to be phrased in such a manner as to question the justice of God. They seem to be implying that it is unfair for people in Old Testament times to go to Hell, when they never had the opportunity to trust Jesus for their salvation; that it is unfair that children could be sent to Hell, simply because they die before they are old enough to trust Jesus for themselves. As we answer these questions, we will see that God maintains His perfection in dealing with both the people of the Old Testament and with children who die prior to reaching an age of understanding. With that being said, let's begin by looking at the topic of salvation in the Old Testament.

SALVATION PRIOR TO JESUS

Jesus clearly states in John 14:6, "I am the way, and the truth, and the life. *No one comes to the Father except through Me*" (emphasis added). Does that mean that no one in the Old Testament could have been saved? Actually, Hebrews 11 is an entire New Testament chapter listing by name *sixteen* Old Testament saints that were saved, in addition to countless unnamed others. The key phrase of the chapter, BY FAITH, gives us a hint as to how they were saved, pointing to the obvious fact that salvation has ALWAYS been by faith in God (Ephesians 2:8). These Old Testament saints believed God's promise to send a Savior. Although they did not meet their Messiah, they trusted God with their salvation. As a result of this faith, they were saved, although their salvation was a bit different than ours in that, based on Jesus's words in Luke 16, it is believed that they were in a different location (Jesus calls it "Abraham's bosom") than those who died without trusting God for their salvation. In other words, they could not ascend directly into the Father's presence because their sins had not been paid for yet. We, on the other hand, who live post-Jesus' resurrection, can enter God's presence immediately upon death, since our debt has been paid (Colossians 2:14).

SALVATION OF CHILDREN

Although the circumstances are totally in the question regarding the salvation of children, the objection is the same. It doesn't seem possible that a child who dies prior to the age of understanding could possibly be saved if Jesus clearly states in John 14:6 that no one comes to the Father except through Him. They never had the opportunity to trust Jesus for their salvation.

Among Christians, there are two views regarding the salvation of children who die before they have the chance to trust Jesus–those who believe the children are saved and those who believe the children are not saved. The lack of consensus is due in part to the fact that there is no specific biblical teaching that addresses the issue. Because there is no clear-cut Bible verse that says all children will be saved, we must approach this topic from a broader perspective.

Given what we know about God and what the Bible does say about children and salvation, a strong case can be made that children who die prior to the age of understanding *are* saved. In support of this conclusion, here are four major truths from God's Word.

- **First**, God is perfectly just. That means God ALWAYS does the right thing. We can trust God to do the right thing, even when we don't see things clearly or understand all that is happening. We can be confident that God would never commit an injustice. If we, as fallen and imperfect moral beings, have enough of a moral sense left in us to know that it would be a grave injustice to condemn innocent infants to Hell, we can trust God's infinitely pure and perfect sense of morality to do the right thing.
- **Second**, Jesus taught that children belong in the Kingdom of Heaven. The words of Jesus are clear when He said, "Let the little children come to me and do not hinder them, for to such belongs the kingdom of heaven" (Matthew 19:14). In the previous chapter of Matthew, Jesus says, "Truly, I say to you, unless you turn and become like children, you will never enter the kingdom of heaven" (Matthew 18:3). These passages, in their context, suggest that children have the innocence and humility required to enter Heaven, and we ought to be more like them in this sense. Paul seems to corroborate this point when addressing the church in Corinth, "Brothers, do not be children in your thinking. Be infants in evil, but in your thinking be mature" (1 Corinithians 14:20). The appeal is to the innocence of children, who lack the deep-seated evil we see in adults.
- **Third**, King David had the conviction that his dead baby was saved. The baby conceived from David's adultery with Bath-sheba was born ill and died within a week. David fasted and prayed for the baby's healing, but it did not come. Once the baby died, David went to the house of the Lord and worshiped. While conversing with his servants, he expresses these words of great hope: "While the child was still alive, I fasted and wept, for I said, 'Who knows whether the Lord will be gracious to me, that the child may live?' But now he is dead. Why should I fast? Can

I bring him back again? **I shall go to him**, but he will not return to me" (2 Samuel 12:22-23). This is not just a reference to the fact that we are all destined to the grave. David expected to be saved by God, as he clearly states: "For you will not abandon my soul to Sheol or let your holy one see corruption. You make known to me the path of life; in your presence there is fullness of joy; at your right hand are pleasures forevermore" (Psalm 16:10-11). Thus, David clearly expected to be reunited with his son in Heaven one day.

- **Fourth**, James believed that sinning involved consciousness of right and wrong. He says, "So whoever knows the right thing to do and fails to do it, for him it is sin" (James 4:17). In the Old Testament, Isaiah seems to make a similar point (Isaiah 7:15). These passages, which are used to argue for an "age of accountability," are considered by many to be the justification for those who die before they can consciously sin. This not only applies to children, but also to mentally handicapped individuals that never really develop a consciousness of sin.

These four truths make for a strong cumulative case for the salvation of children that die before they reach an age of understanding. While one cannot be dogmatic about his position, and every one of these points can be disputed, I believe the case is far more plausible than that of its critics.

CONCLUSION

Does the salvation of Old Testament saints and children prior to the age of accountability bypass the clear teachings of Jesus in John 14:6 that "No one comes to the Father except through me," as some critics argue? Absolutely not.

- Who opened the access door to Heaven? Jesus did.
- Who paid the price of all transgressions? Jesus did.
- Who sits at the right hand of God as our mediator? Jesus does.

If it is possible for anyone, including the two groups considered above, to enter Heaven, it is ONLY because of the finished work of

Jesus. Therefore, the Old Testament saints entered "by the new and living way that Jesus opened for us through the curtain, that is, through His flesh" (Hebrews 10:20). This is the very same access door that infants, children, and the mentally handicapped enter Heaven through. It is the same door we who have trusted Christ for our salvation enter through. There is no other way into Heaven.

Chapter 16

DO YOU REALLY THINK THAT JONAH LIVED IN A WHALE FOR THREE DAYS?

JUAN VALDES

For three decades in a row, the British band, Hot Chocolate, had a hit single with a song that included the lyrics, "*I believe in miracles ...*" STOP! That's the only part of the song I want you to think about. The fundamental "question behind the question" is: Do you believe in miracles?

Before answering, let's define the term "miracle." I'm not talking about the watered-down concept we often throw around so flippantly. When an underdog defeats the best team in town, that's amazing, but it's not a miracle. When you pray for a parking spot near the mall entrance and you find one, that's not a miracle. Incredible as it may seem, even the fact that Betty, the captain of the cheerleading squad, is now dating an unknown freshman named John is not really a miracle. A mystery, yes, but not a miracle. So, before we begin, let's define the word "miracle" as clearly as possible, so that we can consider Jonah's account and determine if it's believable or not.

WHAT IS A MIRACLE?

All definitions are NOT created equal. Many thinkers throughout history have attempted to define miracles. These definitions have been analyzed and criticized, accepted in some cases, and rejected in others, and many of the definitions seem to contradict each other. All this to say that it seems to be quite difficult to define the word "miracle" and to establish the parameters to determine if a given event qualifies as a miracle. Let us consider a couple of well-known definitions.

David Hume, an 18th century skeptic, provided a definition that's still quite popular in textbooks and discussions today. He defined a miracle as "*a violation of the laws of nature*."[61] When confronted with examples of miracles, his response was incredulity (disbelief). He believed that there were events that "looked like a miracle" but if you dug deep enough, you would find a naturalistic explanation, otherwise the event never really happened. Hume's definition is the natural outworking of his worldview. He was an atheist who did not believe in the existence of a supernatural being that created the universe. Thus, from his perspective, the natural world was all that existed. This led him, as it leads other skeptics today, to conclude that everything that occurs in our world MUST have a natural explanation. However, if God does exist, then the entire foundation of Hume's skepticism crumbles, because supernatural explanations then become possible.

Another prominent skeptic (this one from the 17th century) was Baruch Spinoza. He defined miracles as *"contradictions"* and therefore rendered them impossible. He argued that the natural laws could never be violated, and miracles were supposed violations of natural laws, therefore miracles could never actually happen. Interestingly, Spinoza was not an atheist. He did believe in God..."kinda sort of." The difficulty with his position is that his perception of God was not biblical. He was a pantheist—someone who believes God and nature are one and the

---

[61]David Hume, "Of Miracles," *Hume Texts Online*, E 10.36, SBN 127-8. Accessed December 13, 2021. http://davidhume.org/texts/e/ 10#36

same.[62] When Spinoza spoke about natural laws, he was equating them with the very nature of God. Because in his view God is natural law itself, then obviously these laws could never be violated–since God would be acting against his own nature. Thus, Spinoza's worldview excluded miracles by definition–*"a priori."*[63] However, if the God of the Bible exists, He is supernatural by definition and transcends the natural world. That would be devastating to Spinoza's definition since an intervention by God would not constitute a contradiction, because natural law is not equal to God's nature.

These examples make it obvious that one's worldview affects the way one sees everything, including miracles. So, the "question behind the question behind the question" is: "Does the God of the Bible really exist?" If the answer is no, then miracles are not possible. If the answer is yes, then miracles are possible.

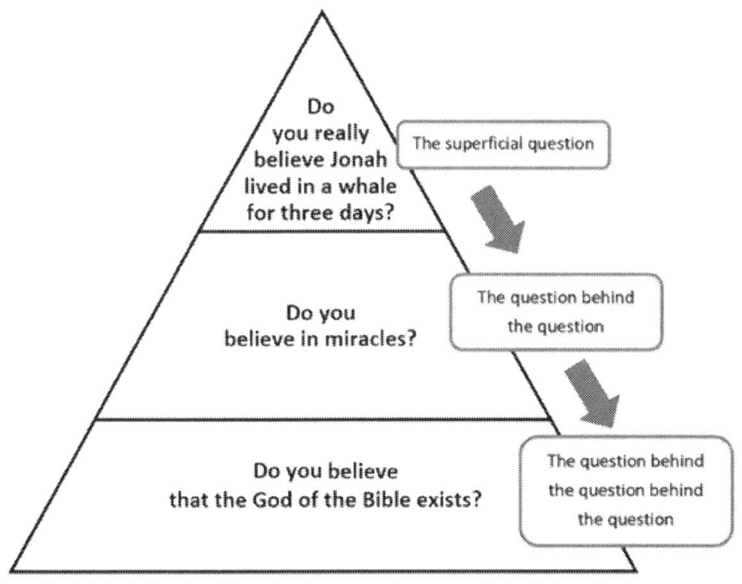

[62]For an in-depth look at Spinoza's definition of miracles, see: *The Chief Works of Benedict de Spinoza, translated from Latin, with an Introduction by R.H.M. Elwes, Vol. 1 Introduction, Tractatus-Theologico-Politicus, Tractatus Politicus. Revised edition* (London: George Bell and Sons, 1891). See https://oll.libertyfund.org/title/elwes-the-chief-works-of-benedict-de-spinoza-vol-1#Spinoza_1321.01_485j (specifically see Chapter VI: Of Miracles).

[63]For an in-depth look at Pantheism in general and to Spinoza's contributions to the ideology, see William Mander and Edward N. Zalta (ed.), "Pantheism," *The Stanford Encyclopedia of Philosophy* (Spring 2020 Edition) at https://plato.stanford.edu/archives/spr2020/entries/pantheism/

Consider some non-skeptical definitions of the word "miracle" as they appear in various English dictionaries. According to Oxford Languages, a miracle is "a surprising and welcome event that is not explicable by natural or scientific laws and is therefore considered to be the work of a divine agency."[64] The Merriam-Webster dictionary has a similar definition: *"an extraordinary event manifesting divine intervention in human affairs."* Lastly, consider this from the Cambridge Dictionary: a miracle is "an unusual and mysterious event that is thought to have been caused by a god because it does not follow the usual laws of nature."

If there were a natural explanation for a "miraculous" event, then it would cease to be a miracle.

All these definitions have something in common: A miracle is an event that cannot be explained naturally and points toward some sort of divine agent. There are good reasons for that—it cannot be explained naturally because it is a supernatural event, and a supernatural event needs a supernatural causal agent. If there were a natural explanation for a "miraculous" event, then it would cease to be a miracle.

Now we come to the nitty-gritty! We can approach this from two directions:

1. We can claim God's existence and prove it by appealing to miracles as supporting evidence (since only God can perform real miracles). However, proving God's existence is not really what we are attempting to do when responding to our question about Jonah. So, we will take the second approach.

2. We can posit that miracles are possible because God exists. In other words, we can use miracles to argue for God's existence, or we can use God's existence to argue for the possibility of miracles.

With that settled, let's address our question: Do we really think

---

[64]For more information, go to https://languages.oup.com/

that Jonah lived in a whale for three days? Absolutely. But let's unpack that.

WHAT ABOUT JONAH'S ACCOUNT?

Imagine if MythBusters did an episode where they set out to prove that the human body cannot survive three days exposed to the acids in the stomach of a whale. The results would be obvious—the stomach acids would probably destroy the human body. I would have no problem agreeing with the results, as it is highly unlikely–maybe even impossible–for a person to survive naturally in that environment for three days. They would end up proving that it seems impossible, naturally speaking. But we have already established that a miracle IS NOT a natural occurrence. If it could happen naturally, it wouldn't be a miracle. The only thing they could possibly prove is that it was not a natural event.

I often come across arguments that attempt to "prove" a miracle didn't happen because it would be naturally impossible. This is a common misconception among skeptics. For example, skeptics argue that Jesus could not have risen from the dead (nor Lazarus, nor the handful of other resurrected people in the Bible) because it's naturally impossible—the body begins decomposing the minute we die. Agreed; bodies don't naturally come back to life after death. But that's why it's considered a miracle! Many argue that Jesus could not walk on water because it violates the laws of nature. Agreed; people cannot naturally walk on water. That's why it's considered a miracle! Water could not possibly be converted into wine because the necessary elements are not present in water. Agreed; water cannot naturally be converted into wine. That's why it's considered a miracle! You get the picture? We should not seek natural explanations for miracles—there are none.

We should not seek natural explanations for miracles—there are none.

So, how can these events take place if they are naturally impossible? Short answer: Supernaturally. However, let's expand on that a little. Think about it with me for a minute. IF there is a God that created the entire universe—the gazillions of stars, the Earth, and the incredible amount of variety of life on Earth, then He designed the very laws that govern the universe He created, revealing them to us in the language of mathematics. How difficult would it be for Him to intervene in the natural world by performing a miracle? Is it more difficult for God to raise a dead man than to create the universe from nothing? You see, once you realize that God exists, miracles are no longer a problem. Keeping Jonah alive inside a huge sea creature is child's play for the all-powerful God of the Bible! Raising Lazarus—restoring his entire biological metabolism—is child's play for the One who designed and created the human body with all its unfathomable complexity!

CONCLUSION

What about the natural laws? Have they been violated by these miracles? Are they no longer valid? OF COURSE NOT! The laws regarding the density of water did not change because Jesus walked on water—go try it out for yourself, and you will see that these laws are intact and working precisely the way God designed them to work. Similarly, the resurrections in the Bible did nothing to undermine or redefine the laws that govern the decomposition of biological matter upon death. **What God did was to intervene at specific times for specific reasons.**

You see, once you realize that God exists, miracles are no longer a problem.

Miracles are not random, supernatural acts. God always has a purpose for performing any given miracle. I believe Jonah lived in a big fish for three days because God miraculously kept him alive. There was a purpose behind the miracle—*Jonah had a mission to complete.*

Chapter 17

HOW CAN I FIGHT AND OVERCOME FEAR?

Candace Nordine

According to the Oxford English dictionary, fear is defined as, *"An unpleasant emotion caused by the belief that someone or something is dangerous, likely to cause pain, or a threat."*

I remember one evening when my husband, Lee, ran to pick up some groceries. Later I heard a knock on the door, and it was a dear friend telling me my husband had been in a car accident. That night, for some reason, I had silenced my cell phone and missed all my husband's calls/texts. My natural response was, of course, fear! Is he ok? Is he dead? Thankfully, he was fine, and God had saved him from serious injury or death. But terrible, bad, ugly things happen in the world around us all the time. Every. Single. Day. You might have what is considered a small fear (fear of bugs), or maybe even something bigger (fear of death), but fear is fear, and it can easily place a stake in your heart and mind and stay planted there.

NO ONE GETS A "PASS" ON FEAR

Often people think they are alone when it comes to fear. However, fear is something that we all experience. It is not selective. No one gets a "pass" from fear in this life. In fact, it's one of the many tools that Satan uses to hinder our trust in the Almighty God. Fear is the very thing that Adam and Eve felt after they sinned against God in the Garden of Eden. "I heard the sound of you in the garden, and I was afraid" (Genesis 3:10). Because sin had now been introduced into God's world, for the first time, fear had reared its ugly head, and we have been feeling the effects ever since. When you experience fear, know that you are not alone. It is such a common emotion to mankind that the Bible tells us over 350 times to "fear not."

TRANSFORM YOUR MIND

The fact is an immediate fearful response is often just a reflection of our fallen nature. There are some weapons we can use in our fight against fear, however, and we can turn fearful situations into an opportunity to grow for God's glory.

1) **Ramp up the attributes of God so that your thoughts just go there**.

Know who God is, that He loves you, that He is for you, and that He limits, orders, and controls all things. Even if you come face to face with your biggest fear, He will give you the grace and mercy to get through even the hardest of times.

The Bible gives us dozens of examples of people who were in very fearful situations, but because they knew and trusted God, they could face what was coming head-on.

- Noah trusted God's warning and promise of provision before the flood.
- David knew God would give him the strength to defeat Goliath.
- Paul faced prison several times, but he knew the God who spoke to him would be with him.

The only way you are going to ramp up, or magnify, the attributes of God is by reading your Bible. You must spend time with someone to get to know them. Jeremiah 9:23-24a reminds us, "Thus says the Lord: 'Let not the wise man boast in his wisdom, let not the mighty man boast in his might, let not the rich man boast in his riches, but let him who boasts boast in this, that he understands and knows me.'"

2) Pray and meditate on Scripture.

Sometimes we simply forget to ask for God's help. We get so caught up in trying to control our own fear that we forget to cry out to God. Make it a practice to pray Scriptures like Isaiah 43:1, "Fear not, for I have redeemed you; I have called you by name, you are mine." One of my favorite Psalms in high school was Psalm 27. It promises that God is my light and my salvation, that I can be confident even when my enemies attack me, and that God will hear my voice when I call out to Him. What great promises! Find your own set of Scriptures that encourage you to focus on who God is and cry out to Him. The more we hide God's Word in our heart, the more it changes our thinking.

3) Develop love.

Some people think the opposite of fear is courage. However, the Bible tells us in 1 John 4:18: "There is no fear in love, but perfect love casts out fear." The antidote to fear is love. When you are fearful, it's harder to be loving. Often when we are fearful, we pull away, or we want to hide, shut down, and take no risk. But a loving person will move forward, give, open up, and risk. The more we love, the more our fear level goes down. We must learn to love from the One who created love. "We love because He first loved us" (1 John 4:19).

The antidote to fear is love.

4) Repent of sin.

Sometimes we are fearful because of unrepentant sin. We are afraid of embarrassment or consequences regarding our sin. However, 1 John 1:9 promises us that "if we confess our sins,

He is faithful and just to forgive us our sins and to cleanse us from all unrighteousness." Yes, it most likely will be hard, but the freedom found in confessing your sin to God will free you from the condemnation you feel. Romans 8:1 says, "Therefore, there is now no condemnation for those who are in Christ Jesus, because through Christ Jesus the law of the Spirit who gives life has set you free from the law of sin and death."

A DIFFERENT KIND OF FEAR

There is another kind of fear, different from the fear of painful circumstances, loss of a loved one, or something creepy like bugs or snakes. This is the fear of man. It's a sneaky kind of fear, and it can be the most threatening to your walk with God. Instead of seeing the incredible worth and value that God sees in you, you look for the approval of others, crave their honor and recognition, and fear their criticism. This desire to be affirmed by others can lead to low self-confidence and self-worth and often makes you timid when you should be bold. It may even cause you to be unstable in your faith. The writer of Proverbs calls the fear of man a snare. "The fear of man lays a snare, but whoever trusts in the Lord is safe" (Proverbs 29:25). This snare (or trap) can often motivate our behavior to do things that are unbiblical.

A HEALTHY KIND OF FEAR

Proverbs 1:7 states, "The fear of the Lord is the beginning of knowledge." It is apparent that the writer doesn't want you to forget to fear the Lord because he repeats it in chapters 9, 10, 14, 15, 20, etc.–you get the point. But what does it actually mean for us to fear God? It means that we have an awe and reverence for God and that we fully surrender to the almighty Creator of the universe. It's something God asks of us. Deuteronomy 10:12 says, "And now, Israel, what does the Lord your God require of you, but to fear the Lord your God, to walk in all His ways, to love Him, to serve the Lord your God with all your heart and with all your soul." This doesn't mean we should

Rather, our awe, reverence, and respect for Him should impact how we live our lives.

be afraid of God. Rather, our awe, reverence, and respect for Him should impact how we live our lives. God loves us and He promises in Romans that nothing can separate us from His love (Romans 8:38-39).

WHAT DOES JESUS SAY ABOUT FEAR?

Jesus talks about fear twice in the Gospels–once in Matthew and once in Luke, and they essentially say the same thing. Here's what Matthew 10:28 says: "And do not fear those who kill the body but cannot kill the soul. Rather fear Him who can destroy both soul and body in Hell."

The thing we truly have to fear is separation from a holy God for all eternity. He sent Jesus, His only Son. Jesus took our place on the cross, and He took the punishment for our sin. Because of that sacrifice, we no longer have to fear separation from God. If we put our faith and trust in Him, we have the promise of eternity with Him in Heaven. If you know Jesus, you will never have to fear death or separation from Him.

CONCLUSION

If you were to ask me whether I experienced fear on the day of Lee's accident, I would say, "Yes, I was fearful." However, I knew even in that moment of fear that God was going to be with us. I knew this because I had seen His faithfulness before. Several years earlier Lee had fallen almost twenty feet through a ceiling, and God had spared his life. Through this previous experience, I had learned to trust God. I had seen and experienced that all things work together for our good and His Glory (Romans 8:28). This doesn't mean I will never again respond in fear when faced with scary circumstances. Every day, in big and small ways, I experience the temptation to take my eyes off God and look instead at the winds and waves around me, but the goal is to fear *less*. I can know who God is; I can trust Him completely, and you can, too.

Chapter 18

WHY DO MY PARENTS FEEL LIKE THEY NEED TO SHOVE CHRISTIANITY DOWN MY THROAT?

DAVE GLANDER

Most people would rather go through life without anyone really "getting in their business." While this may sound ideal, is it really? Penn Jillette, mentioned in an earlier chapter, is a well-known magician in Las Vegas … but he is also well-known as one of the most arrogant, outspoken atheists alive today. Some years ago, he posted a video talking about his encounter with a Christian who had attended one of his shows. Afterward, the man gave him a Bible and attempted to tell him about Jesus. Considering how hostile Penn is about faith in general, I was shocked to see that he was not angry or upset that the person would have the audacity to share his faith. Here are his thoughts about their encounter:

> I've always said that I don't respect people who don't proselytize [share their faith]. I don't respect that at all. If you believe

> that there's a Heaven and a Hell, and people could be going to Hell or not getting eternal life, and you think that it's not really worth telling them this because it would make it socially awkward..., how much do you have to hate somebody to not proselytize? How much do you have to hate somebody to believe everlasting life is possible and not tell them that? I mean, if I believed, beyond the shadow of a doubt, that a truck was coming at you, and you didn't believe that truck was bearing down on you, there is a certain point where I tackle you. And this is more important than that.[65]

SOMETIMES, THE TRUTH HURTS

What would life truly be like if nobody loved us enough to tell us something that may be difficult to hear? What if nobody cared enough to tell a drug addict that there's a way out, or a gambling addict that there is hope for him to get his life back together? The fact is that it's easier to just turn a blind eye and not get involved. However, genuinely loving someone means being there for them through all of life's highs and lows. It's easy to love somebody when everything is going great, but do you love them enough to tell them the truth about a decision they are making that may harm them?

TRUTH IS TRUE, EVEN IF NOBODY BELIEVES IT. A LIE IS A LIE, EVEN IF EVERYONE BELIEVES IT!

While the subject of truth can (and did) occupy an entire chapter on its own, it's critical that we at least touch on the topic for a moment so that we can fully understand why it is important to share it. Truth is not a concept, or a feeling, or a philosophical argument. Truth is founded in the very person of Jesus Christ who said, "I am the Way, the TRUTH, and the Life" (John 14:6a).

Truth is true for ALL people, in ALL places, at ALL times. An example of that can be found in the statement: "We all need food to live." Everyone who has ever lived in any location around the globe all need(ed) food to live. There has never been a person that lived without eating.

---

[65]ChurchPOP Editor, "Atheist Penn Jillette Doesn't Respect Christians Who Don't Evangelize," *ChurchPOP*, January 16, 2016. For the full story and video, please go to https://www.churchpop.com/ 2016/01/16/atheist-penn-jillette-christians-evangelize/

Another truth is the ultimate reality of death. Every person who has ever lived (except Enoch–Genesis 5:24–and Elijah–2 Kings 2:1-12) has faced death or will face death eventually, and no one can escape that reality. The Bible says it is appointed for "man to die once, and then after that comes judgment" (Hebrews 9:27). Death is as real as the air you breathe. The truth is there is an afterlife. You possess an eternal soul that will face inevitable judgment concerning the days you lived while on Earth. Jesus didn't only say He is the Truth, He also said He is the **WAY**. He followed that up with, "No one comes to the Father except through me" (John 14:6b).

It's easy to love somebody when everything is going great, but do you love them enough to tell them the truth about a decision they are making that may harm them?

For the sake of argument, let's return to the statement from Penn Jillette. If your parents really believe the Christian doctrine that there is an afterlife, and that you will be judged when you get there, and that the only way to avoid a place called Hell is to be saved by Jesus, how much would your parents have to hate you to not try to share that with you? It may not be what you want to hear, but it is because of their immense love that they feel convicted to share the information with you.

I am convinced that one of the main reasons for parents wanting their kids to understand the Christian faith so desperately is because they know that if their kids give their lives to Jesus Christ, they will be safe and secure for eternity in His hands. You see, Jesus didn't just say He is the Way, and the Truth, He also said He is the **LIFE**! Isaiah 49:8 (NKJV) says, "… in the day of salvation I have helped you; I will preserve you."

Did you just read that? What parent wouldn't want that for their own children? A real Christian parent understands that Jesus isn't some kind of fire insurance. No, they understand that Jesus offers "life, and to have it more abundantly" (John 10:10b). The Greek word translated *"abundantly"* literally means *"more, greater, excessive, abundant, exceedingly, vehemently"*; it's an amazing life!

Christian parents understand that when their child trusts Jesus as their personal Savior, not only is their eternal soul secure with God forever, but that "forever" starts immediately. They understand that as their kids grow in the knowledge of our God, He will bring them a more exceedingly abundant life! What kind of a parent would stay silent with that kind of knowledge? How bad would that parent have to hate their child to not remind them as often as possible? The proper response for a parent who loves their kid would *absolutely* be to talk to them about Jesus.

COMMUNICATION BREAKDOWN

I've been in youth ministry for a long time and have noticed how many kids have a bad drug problem. No, not *that* kind of drug problem. I've seen kids "drug" to church without any explanation as to why. Unfortunately, some parents don't know how to properly communicate the importance of the Christian faith, so they drag their kids to church with the hope that one of the pastors will have success with them. It is important that the reader understand that while there may be a breakdown in a parent's ability to properly communicate, love is what's driving them to drag their kids to church every week.

> *The proper response for a parent who loves their kid would* ***absolutely*** *be to talk to them about Jesus.*

Sometimes parents aren't the best at communication. Heck, we're all guilty of that charge at various times of our lives. But the last time I checked, bad communication has never changed the actual truth of the message: A message can remain true whether communicated properly or not.

CONCLUSION

When a parent loves their child, they will do anything for them. I have seen parents bend over backwards to make sure their kids have everything they need to succeed at sports or in school. I have also seen some parents who could care less about the health of their kids to the point that they allow their kids to do whatever they want. The latter never turns out very well for the kid.

When I was an atheist living in the world, I desperately wanted to be a famous musician. In order to achieve the goals of growing into a musician, I surrounded myself with like-minded people in all areas of the music world. I sought after fellow musicians, publishers, writers, groupies, managers, talent scouts, vendors, booking agents, etc. The best way to get *where* you want to be is to surround yourself with everything associated with *what* you are trying to be.

In the end, I don't think the question is WHY would a parent be so exhaustive in making sure their child knows Jesus... the real question is why WOULDN'T they?

When a parent truly understands the nature of God, both now and forever, it is only natural that the parent should also bend over backwards to make sure that their child has everything necessary to succeed in life.

- They should make sure they are praying with them daily.
- They should do a Bible devotion with them daily.
- They should help them answer questions that come up about their faith.
- They should make sure that they are in church, with like-minded folks, on a very regular basis.
- They should make sure that their child gets plugged into some kind of ministry that their child can thrive and grow in.

In the end, I don't think the question is WHY would a parent be so exhaustive in making sure their child knows Jesus … the real question is why WOULDN'T they? The next time your parents try to tell you about Jesus, thank them for the love they are showing to you, even if you may not agree with them!

PART FOUR

BIBLICAL ANSWERS

Chapter 19

HOW DO WE DEAL WITH DEATH?

JUAN VALDES

Dealing with death is one of the hardest things we do in life. Thus, dealing with this question is important to all of us. Having suffered the loss of my dad and the death of close relatives and friends, in addition to having officiated countless funeral and burial services, there is one question that stands out to me: Why does it hurt so much? We grope for how to deal with such a high level of pain and heartbreak. As we consider this question, we need to deal with three interrelated issues. First, it is important to establish why the death of a loved one is so incredibly painful. This helps us understand the pain. Second, we need to understand how to deal with the death of a loved one. Finally, we must understand how to deal with the inevitable prospect of our own death.

WHY IS DEATH SO PAINFUL AND HEARTBREAKING?

Ruppert H. McTruell died last month in Fenwick, Connecticut. How does that make you feel? Honestly, did it bring you to tears? Probably not. Did the news elicit any form of grief? Probably not. Why is it that the death of some people breaks us with unbearable grief while the death of others has absolutely no impact whatsoever? Now, don't beat yourself up for not crying over Ruppert's death; you're not a monster. It is perfectly normal human behavior not to feel a sense of loss when someone we don't know passes away, because the key difference is LOVE. Our love for someone is the reason why some deaths hurt, and others don't. Love is the reason we suffer immense grief when dealing with the death of *a loved one*.

Now that we know what's causing the pain, the solution should be relatively easy. The way to rid ourselves of the pain would simply be to stop loving, right? Even if that were possible, I can assure you it's not a good strategy. Since we are made in the image of God, we are designed to love. It's what ultimately defines the nature of an ideal relationship with God and with each other. That's why love is at the center of the two greatest commandments (Matthew 22:37-39).

It was God's perfect plan in Eden for mankind to love Him and each other with everything we've got. In Eden, that love would never have resulted in pain, suffering, heartbreak, or grief. Were it not for sin, death would not have entered our creation (Romans 5:12). No death = no grief. One day it will be that way again, but in the meantime, it's not like that!

HOW CAN WE DEAL WITH THE DEATH OF A LOVED ONE?

There are many ways to deal with grief. When my dad passed away, I was 23 years old, married, had my own apartment, and a beautiful one year old baby daughter ... yet my dad's passing was devastating to me. He wasn't only my dad; he was my best friend in the world. We did everything together: fishing, motorcycling, church–everything. As a Christian, I knew he was with the Lord, but my head and my heart were on different pages. Knowing that a loved one is in Heaven is a tremendous comfort, but it doesn't take away the emotional pain of the loss. To deal with the pain, I found incredible relief by visiting the cemetery, sitting next to his tombstone, and talking to him. I know, I know, he wasn't there, but I had so much I needed to express to him that I poured out my soul, and I cried. I would walk away numb yet feeling a certain level of relief. I don't recall how long this went on, but it was probably a few weeks. Then, one day, I stopped visiting the cemetery. I felt I had released enough of my pain that I could now bear the grief that was left. I'm not suggesting this is the solution for anyone else. Some grieve by taking on new projects and occupying their minds on new things. Others find relief in counseling or just having someone listen to them. The point is that everyone grieves differently. In addition, there is no set time limit for grief. Some people feel better in a matter of months; for others it takes years. It is also important to know that *it is okay to cry and to grieve*. After all, even Jesus cried over the death of his friend Lazarus!

Giving ourselves room to grieve is important, however, we must be careful not to surrender completely to grief. What I mean is that, if allowed, grief can take over our lives and lead us to depression, thoughts of suicide, and even physical illness. As difficult as it may be to do, we must continue to live. We must learn to live with the pain, because it never really goes away. We never stop loving those that have gone before us, but it does get better. With time, we learn to adapt to life without our loved one. We still miss them, but the pain is no longer paralyzing. One of the secrets is to focus on making the best of the life we have been given. We have the privilege of being alive and carrying out the mission God has assigned us. Surely our loved ones would not want us to waste the wonderful gift of life. Sooner or later, though, we ourselves will also face death and we must prepare ourselves for that reality.

Knowing that a loved one is in Heaven is a tremendous comfort, but it doesn't take away the emotional pain of the loss.

HOW CAN WE DEAL WITH THE PROSPECTS OF OUR OWN DEATH?

Our own death, for obvious reasons, must be approached differently than that of someone we love. For most people, the prospect of death seems so remote that it doesn't merit any immediate attention. Despite the fact that nobody is guaranteed another breath, we often approach our daily lives with the illusion that we still have plenty of time left. Every day, people of all ages leave this world. As Christians, we should live our lives accordingly. Embracing this allows us to prepare for the inevitability of the death of our mortal bodies. But what if you're not a Christian? How should you prepare?

First, you should take care of our reservations on the other side. The Bible is clear that we as humans are composed of two parts, one physical (our body) and one spiritual (our soul). When our physical body dies, our soul continues to exist. That means that the moment we take our last physical breath, we enter eternity. The Bible is also clear that there are only two places to choose between on the map of "the other side." We can either spend the rest of our lives in Heaven with God and all the redeemed that have preceded us, or we can spend the rest of our lives in Hell with Satan and all the lost souls. In dealing with the prospect of our own death, NOTHING can be more pressing than settling this NOW. We have the option to choose in this life where we will spend eternity. What a privilege that is! We can choose to trust Jesus for our salvation and be assured of eternal life in Heaven. But sadly, there is another option: We can choose to reject Jesus and spend eternity without Him—not a good idea. It is also noteworthy that if you die without deciding in this life, the default destination is Hell. This is because we have all fallen short of the glory of God and the wages of our sins is death—eternal separation from God (Romans 3:23; 6:23).

Every day, people all around us step into eternity unprepared.

Second, we should make it a priority to share with others about the wonderful opportunity we have to get right with God. Without a doubt, our greatest earthly mission is speaking to the lost about where they stand before a holy God and explaining what He did so that we can be made right with Him. Every day, people all around us step into eternity unprepared. We need to make it a priority in our lives to minimize those numbers. In other words, part of how we deal with the prospect of our own death is by taking advantage of whatever time we've got left to make a difference in the lives of others.

Third, we should value every day as a precious gift from God. Don't let a single day go to waste. Live every day as if it were your last day on Earth, for one day it will be. Love and enjoy every second you have with your loved ones. Finally, for those who are blessed to know when death is coming, don't worry about those that are left behind—God will take care of them. After all, isn't He the one that has always taken care of them? Settle your affairs and try to enjoy every second you have with your loved ones.

CONCLUSION

Dealing with death is not easy, but it is a part of life in this fallen world. However, as Paul taught the Thessalonians, we don't grieve as those without any hope. We are a people of hope. Jesus' words in John 11:25-26 should be a constant source of comfort: "I am the resurrection and the life. Whoever believes in me, though he die, yet shall he live, and everyone who lives and believes in me shall never die."

Chapter 20

IS HELL REALLY FOREVER?

BUB KUNS

Hell is a serious subject, and the Bible has much to say about it. Before we get into this particular question, however, please note that this is certainly not meant to be an exhaustive treatise on the topic and reality of Hell. We are not going to get into in-depth details, nor are we going to attempt to explain the exact differences between the various words and idioms used to describe Hell. Our main focus here is on the question at hand, namely, "Is Hell Really Forever?"

There are varying views on this topic, but what I call the Big 4 are as follows:

1) There is no Hell. (The No-Hell View)

2) There's a Hell, but it's only for demons and Satan. (Universal Salvation View)

3) Hell is real but not eternal. (The Conditional View)

4) Hell is a place of eternal torment. (Traditional View)

Let's take a brief look at each of these views and compare them to Scripture. As we begin, let's look at the most popular and descriptive verses on the topic.

VERSES TO CONSIDER

(Words in **bold** print indicate emphasis added.)

> "And many of those who sleep in the dust of the Earth shall awake, **some to everlasting life**, and **some to shame and everlasting contempt**" (Daniel 12:2).
>
> "And do not fear those who kill the body but cannot kill the soul. Rather fear him who can destroy both soul and body **in hell**" (Matthew 10:28).
>
> "Just as the weeds are gathered and burned with fire, so **will it be at the end of the age**. The Son of Man will send his angels, and they will gather out of his kingdom all causes of sin and all lawbreakers and **throw them into the fiery furnace. In that place there will be weeping and gnashing of teeth**" (Matthew 13:40–42).
>
> "And these will go **away into eternal punishment**, but the righteous into eternal life" (Matthew 25:46).
>
> "They will suffer the **punishment of eternal destruction**, **away from the presence of the Lord** and from the glory of his might" (2 Thessalonians 1:9).
>
> "And if anyone's name was not found written in the book of life, he was **thrown into the lake of fire**" (Revelation 20:15).

No doubt, there are many other verses having to do with Hell, but these should suffice. Having read the verses above, let's now explore the "Big 4."

THE NO-HELL VIEW: "THERE ISN'T REALLY A HELL."

This view has no Scriptural support. It's been made popular by atheists, materialists, and some "Christians" who, for reasons more emotional than scriptural, can't seem to (or don't want to) reconcile a God of love and the idea of any kind of everlasting punishment. However, emotions are not a reliable source of truth. Instead of allowing our emotions to get the best of us, we must rely on Scripture to guide, train, and correct us even though what we hear or read might seem unpleasant or be beyond our understanding. We cannot attempt to erase Hell for emotional or preferential reasons because doing so is dangerous to the Gospel and is not biblical.

A Real Place for Real People

When one reads words like "**in** Hell," or "throw them **into** the **fiery furnace**," or "**in that place**," or "**into** the lake of fire," it seems unreasonable to conclude that there is no real place into which anyone is being thrown. In fact, almost every verse about Hell describes a real place, with real torment, happening to real beings. From just the few verses above, we know that, at the very least, some people receive everlasting life, and some will be held in everlasting contempt. We know that bodies are thrown into an actual place called "Hell" (from the Greek, *Gehenna*, a place once celebrated for the awful worship of Moloch where the stench, flames and carcasses of dead bodies and extreme filth existed) which is synonymous (at least for the purposes of this chapter) with a "lake of fire," or "fiery furnace" where actual people are "away from the presence of the Lord." We further understand that there will be "weeping and gnashing of teeth" and "they will suffer the punishment of eternal destruction." If Hell is simply metaphorical, all these descriptions and references to an actual location become senseless.

To be fair, the language describing the actual place may be figurative or metaphorical, but that only further supports the truth that Hell is an actual, real place, because it would make no sense to use metaphors and descriptive language for a place that doesn't exist. The point of the language is for us to understand that it's a real place, and it's horrible. If Hell doesn't exist, describing it like this would be nonsensical. For this and for many other reasons, most scholars and serious students of Scripture reject this view.

Summary of the No-Hell View

The most common form of this belief is that God won't ultimately discipline or punish those who are dead in their sins and trespasses and who reject Christ's free gift of salvation, but instead that God's love brings all to Him. A God of love would never create a Hell-like place or enact divine retribution. The short answer to the question, "Is Hell

Really Forever" from the No-Hell view is, "No, it's not forever, because Hell doesn't exist."

UNIVERSAL SALVATION VIEW: "EVERYBODY MAKES IT TO HEAVEN … EVENTUALLY."

The most common universalist belief is that eventually ALL will be saved, and that Hell is temporary for people and permanent only for Satan and demons. Note that they do not reject the existence of Hell, nor divine retribution; but they do reject the notion that it's an eternal place for people. They hold that Hell is a place used by God to bring all to repentance and salvation, except the Devil and the demons, who are condemned to eternal conscious torment in the lake of fire.

While no biblical passages implicitly or explicitly establish universalism, the universalists support their position by citing the following verses (among others):

> "Then he will say to those on his left, 'Depart from me, you cursed, into eternal fire **prepared for the devil and his angels'"** (Matthew 25:41).

> "For in him [Christ] all the fullness of God was pleased to dwell, and through Him to reconcile to himself **all things**, whether on Earth or in heaven, making peace by the blood of his cross" (Colossians 1:19-20).

> "Then as one man's trespass led to condemnation **for all men**, so one man's act of righteousness leads to acquittal and life **for all men**. For as by one man's disobedience **many were made sinners**, so by one man's obedience **many will be righteous**" (Romans 5:18).

> "For as in Adam **all die**, so also in Christ shall a**ll be made alive**" (1 Corinthians 15:22).

Summary of Universalism

According to the "Universalist View," there are two categories of people–those who are saved on Earth by the grace of Christ and after death, they go to heaven (they never enter Hell); and those who are not saved on Earth, but through some form of discipline in Hell, end up repenting and being saved. Ultimately only Satan and the demons will be forever tormented in an everlasting Hell, though some universalists believe that eventually Satan and the demons will be obliterated. This view is categorically rejected by most Christian scholars because it is found nowhere in Scripture. Quite the contrary, most of the passages listed, when considered in their respective context, end up refuting universalism.

Thus, the short answer to the question, "Is Hell really forever?" from the "Universalist View" would be, "No, it's not forever (for people), but it may be for Satan and the demons."

THE CONDITIONAL VIEW: "HELL IS REAL BUT TEMPORARY."

A view that is gaining in popularity is the "Conditional View," often called the conditional immortality view. The most common belief of conditionalists is that Hell is not eternal because ultimately all evil (all those not saved by the grace of Jesus), Satan and demons are all eventually annihilated–completely obliterated into non-existence. They do NOT deny the doctrine of Hell or its existence. They hold to divine wrath for the unsaved and to complete and utter destruction of any and all evil in the end.

The reason it is often called conditional immortality is because proponents of this view hold that only the saved are granted eternal life (immortality) while the unsaved have a period of punishment, but are eventually annihilated–that is, they completely cease to exist. They hold that all references to "eternal" or "everlasting" punishment and/or torment are indeed "everlasting" because ultimately, one ceases to exist. If you don't exist, you don't exist "forever." Therefore, your non-existence is eternal punishment.

Defining terms this way means that you can take all the verses we listed at the opening of this chapter (and others), play them out under this view, and find that Scripture is not violated. Take the popular John 3:16 passage: "For God so loved the world that He gave His only begotten Son, so that whoever believes in Him shall **not perish** but **have eternal life.**" For the conditionalist, there are two opposites here–death and life. There are those who ultimately perish (die forever) and those who are granted eternal life (live forever). One is eternally dead, and another is eternally alive. One of the biggest problems with this view and the way it interprets eternal death is that the Bible also speaks of eternal fire and eternal torment associated with Hell. Neither of these concepts fits into the reinterpretation of eternal punishment proposed by this view.

As far as being thrown in a lake of fire, or a fiery furnace, or a place where there is weeping and gnashing of teeth, the conditionalist would agree, but they just don't believe it's forever. As far as the wrath of God being poured out on those dead in their sins and their denial of Jesus, the conditionalist agrees; they just don't believe it's eternal conscious torment. They hold fast to Scripture as God's inerrant Word and believe salvation comes only by the grace of Jesus through faith. The challenge they propose is for us to understand and interpret words like "eternal" and "everlasting" as words connoting finality of judgment in and of themselves. However, this connotation of finality of judgment is inconsistent with what we find in Scripture.

Summary of the Conditionalist View

The short answer to the question "Is Hell Really Forever?" from a conditionalist is, "No. It's real and it's horrible, and there are different forms and durations of punishment, but ultimately all who are there, and Hell itself, will one day cease to exist completely." This goes for Satan and the demons–they will be utterly annihilated as well. Eventually there will be no remnant of evil in any part of the universe. This sounds amazing, yet it is not a biblical view of how everything ends.

THE TRADITIONAL VIEW: "ETERNAL, CONSCIOUS TORMENT"

By far the most popular view among main-stream evangelical Christians, church pastors, and teachers over the last millennia is that Hell is a place of eternal, conscious torment with gradations of torment depending on the deeds of those who end up there. Let me clearly state that popularity alone isn't a reliable source of truth; I only bring it up so that you understand that thousands of faithful people have studied this topic over the years and hold to the idea of eternal, conscious torment based on Scripture.

Certainly, a plain reading of Scripture on the topic of Hell seems to indicate some kind of conscious torment in an unpleasant place that apparently goes on forever. Jesus's account of the rich man and Lazarus in Luke 16:19-31 seems to indicate that a real rich man ends up in Hades (Hell) which is described as a place of "anguish in this flame." This rich man asks for Abraham to send Lazarus (who is not in Hell) to "dip the end of his finger and cool [his] tongue…" But Abraham refuses and reminds him that the rich man is in one place, and Abraham and Lazarus are in another, and between them is a "great chasm that has been fixed, in order that those who would pass from here to you may not be able, and no one may cross from there to us." The place where Abraham and Lazarus are is everlasting, which seems to indicate that the place where the rich man is in is also everlasting.

Daniel 12:2 states, "And many of those who sleep in the dust of the Earth shall awake, **some to everlasting life**, and **some to shame and everlasting contempt."** Again, a plain reading of this verse suggests that the contempt some will awake to is "everlasting." Now to be fair, the culture in which Daniel wrote this was a shame-based culture that put a lot of emphasis on how one will be remembered after death. The second part of the verse could be a reference that some will be thought of forever as horribly contemptible. But it seems a bit of a stretch, as the verse seems to be comparing "everlasting life" and "everlasting contempt" in the form of final judgment.

One last example (since we don't have space here to tackle this issue comprehensively) is Revelation 20:10. It states, "and the devil who had deceived them was thrown into the lake of fire and sulfur where the beast and the false prophet were, and they will be tormented **day and night forever and ever**." It appears that ultimately the devil (a fallen angelic being), the beast (most likely a political leader over a beastly empire), and the false prophet (presumably a human) are literally "thrown into the lake of fire and sulfur" where they will "be tormented day and night forever and ever." The language here is quite emphatic, and the combination of the terms "day and night" and "forever and ever" seems to reinforce eternal, conscious torment. Again, though, to be fair, this could only be relating to those three beings, and not others. But it still seems that ultimately those three entities will endure eternal, conscious punishment in an ongoing, eternal manner, which means they are not annihilated.

Summary of Traditional View

This view holds that all people not saved by the grace of Jesus Christ on Earth will be cast into Hell where there will be eternal, conscious punishment of varying degrees. Those not in Christ are dead in their sins and trespasses, guilty of a multitude of sins which have not been paid for, and guilty of rejecting the work of Jesus Christ as the only propitiation (appeasement) for their sin. Thus, their sins against an eternal God must be paid for eternally. The short answer to the question "Is Hell Really Forever?" from a traditional view is, "Yes. It's a terrible place of everlasting, conscious torment."

CONCLUSION

Hell is an uncomfortable and tough subject to talk about for most people, but God, in His infinite wisdom, chose to put many references about it in His Holy Word. We need to respect that and commit to reading Scripture and taking our direction from it. Any view on Hell that is not from God's Word is not worth accepting or pursuing. Any view on Hell that does not account for the full counsel of God's Word on the topic should also be rejected. Thus, the traditional view is left as the strongest of the aforementioned views that accounts for all that the Bible says on Hell. So then, Christians, whether we hold to the traditional view or not, we should be motivated to share the loving truth of the Gospel so that as many as possible will never have to experience the horrors of Hell.

Chapter 21

WERE THE DAYS IN GENESIS REALLY "DAYS"?

Carl Kerby

Some people argue that the six days of creation in Genesis 1 don't have to be literal 24-hour days because "a verse, somewhere in the New Testament, says that a day is like a thousand years." If this is the case, they argue, then the "days" in Genesis can be long periods of time.

ARE THE "DAYS" OF GENESIS DIFFERENT FROM GOD'S PERSPECTIVE?

Actually, the verse they're referring to, 2 Peter 3:8, has nothing to do with the days in Genesis. The verse says that "*with the Lord* one day is as a thousand years, *and* a thousand years as one day" (emphasis added). To understand verse 8 in context, you need to read 2 Peter 3:1-7, where the author teaches that Genesis is actual history and warns that in the last days scoffers are going to come along and mock the truth of that history. He then uses the illustration in verse 8 to show that God is not restricted by time; instead, He is the CREATOR of time. He therefore exists outside the dimension of time and is not bound by its limitations. That's why it says "with the Lord"—meaning from His perspective, outside of time—a thousand years and a day are the same. Likewise, Psalm 90:4 tells us, "For in your sight a thousand years are like yesterday that passes by, like a few hours of the night." This reference to days and years has nothing whatsoever to do with the days found in the Genesis account.

Those who try to make the days of creation more than a 24-hour day would never use the 2 Peter verse to teach that the three days from the cross to the resurrection were equal to three thousand years. In addition, they ignore the second part of the verse. They would never say that the (approximately) 2,000-year period from Abraham to the cross was only two days. The bottom line is that they have taken the verse out of context to try to make it say what they want it to say, as a way to fit "science" (i.e., current evolutionary teaching) into the Bible. Furthermore, the Hebrew word used for "day" in Genesis is the word *"yom,"* and when the word *yom* is used:

- With a number (410 times), it always means an ordinary 24-hour day.
- With "evening" **and** "morning" (38 times), it always means an ordinary 24-hour day.
- With "evening" **or** "morning" (27 times), it always means an ordinary 24-hour day.
- With "night" (52 times), it always means an ordinary 24-hour day.

Why, then, would the use of *yom* in the creation account in Genesis 1 be an exception? Jesus quoted Genesis over twenty times in the New Testament (for example, Luke 24:13-25; Matthew 4; Matthew 19:4,5; Mark 10:6) and EVERY time He did so, He quoted it as an actual, historical account and not allegory, poetry, or fairy tale. Christ also modeled for us that Scripture is where we should be looking for answers.

Finally, the Scripture is abundantly clear that the days in Genesis are the same length as we know days to be today. God used the seven days of creation to be a pattern for how modern man would use time: "In six days the LORD made the heavens and the Earth, the sea, and all that is in them, and rested the seventh day. Therefore, the LORD blessed the Sabbath day and hallowed it" (Exodus 20:11).

Think about it: This truth is so powerful that it's the foundation for our calendar week. Our days, months, and years are based on what we observe in the natural world (the movements of the sun, Earth, and moon) … but the basis for our week is found first in God's Word.

DOES "SCIENCE" REALLY PROVE THE EARTH IS MILLIONS OF YEARS OLD?

Remember, Jesus is the Creator of all things (John 1:1-3; Colossians 1:16). He should know how, why, and when it all happened and in what sequence. Adam and Eve were created "from the beginning." It's therefore impossible to biblically justify millions of years of death and suffering occurring before the creation of man and woman. You cannot biblically support millions of years of death and suffering *before* Adam was created.

Why, you ask? Romans 6:23 tells us that "the wages of sin is death." Also, the book of Romans clearly states that by one man sin entered the world (Romans 5:12,19), and because of sin, we see death (Romans 5:12). If the Genesis days were long ages of evolution, as some claim, then that would mean that during those millions of years before Adam's existence (and his sin), there was already death and suffering.

Why are we so willing to sell out Jesus, the Creator of EVERYTHING, for a belief system that changes every time a new rock is found somewhere?

People claim that "Science proves the Earth is millions of years old!" Sorry, but no, it does not! Sometimes when I speak, I'll ask, *"Do the biology textbooks in schools today teach the same thing as textbooks 10 years ago? 20 years ago? 50 years ago? 100 years ago?"* Every time the audience will respond with a resounding "No!" to each of those examples. I'll then ask, *"Does the Bible that you're holding teach the same thing as 10 years ago? 20 years ago? 50 years ago? 100 years ago?"* This response is always, "Yes!" Why are we so willing to sell out Jesus, the Creator of EVERYTHING, for a belief system that changes every time a new rock is found somewhere? Think about it: If everything that they "know" to be true right now can be totally eliminated with one new rock, how strong is their position?

If you think that I'm exaggerating, please allow me to give you a very specific example that just happened at the time of this writing. In my first draft for this response, I had cited an article from the BBC Earth.com website originally published on November 2, 2015. It read:

"Meet a lamprey. Your ancestors looked just like it"[66]

In this article was the following statement: *"These primitive fish have existed in a virtually unchanged form for an amazingly long time. Fossil lampreys that look essentially identical to modern species date back to 360 million years."*

While scientific findings often contradict evolutionistic claims, God is the same yesterday, today, and forever (Hebrews 13:8).

You might say, "There you go, Carl, 'science' proves we go back millions of years!" My response is: "Be patient, give 'science' time and it will catch up with reality." Fast-forward to the year 2021, and we have a new headline:

"Long-accepted theory of vertebrate origin upended by fossilized fish larvae"[67]

These researchers now say that what has been taught as fact–by evolutionists–for 150 years (that we could have evolved from fish larvae) is no longer true! You might be asking, *"Why would he go into all that when talking about the days in Genesis?"* That's a very good question, and here's why: This is a prime example of where scientists must change everything that they think to be true because of new evidence. The bottom line is science does not prove a long age for the Earth.

---

[66]Colin Barras, "Meet a lamprey. Your ancestor looked just like it," *BBC Earth*, November 2, 2015. https://colinbarras.couk/2015/11/02/meet-a-lamprey-your-ancestors-looked-just-like-it/

[67]University of Chicago Medical Center, "Long-accepted theory of vertebrate origin upended by fossilized fish larvae," PHYS.ORG (March 10, 2021). https://phys.org/news/2021-03-long-accepted-theory-vertebrate-upendedfossilized.html?fbclid=IwAR0iXv_nuo9ZM1R49qd9m8VF66FuujH-iDpUvL_1uXDITzA38XVNFt-SbUk

By the way, BBC Earth has removed the article about the lamprey from their site. You can only find an abbreviated version of it on the actual author's site (which I have footnoted). While scientific findings often contradict evolutionistic claims, God is the same yesterday, today, and forever (Hebrews 13:8).

CONCLUSION

We have seen that the language in Genesis 1, as well as supporting Scriptures, makes it evident that the days spoken of are literal 24-hour days. God clearly stated *exactly* what He meant, so you don't have to be confused. What the world is teaching does not and cannot mesh with His Word and just doesn't make sense!

Please don't try to apply "man's wisdom" to God's Word and tell Him what He meant because of a false assumption that He doesn't understand science. Just do as He commands in Proverbs 3:5: "Trust in the LORD with all your heart, and do not lean on your own understanding."

Chapter 22

AREN'T THERE CONTRADICTIONS IN THE GOSPELS?

Frank Figueroa

Non-believers and skeptics often claim that the Bible is full of errors. If you are a believer, you will probably be asked this question by a skeptic at some point in your life. Are you prepared to answer it? An initial way to engage in this conversation would be to ask, "Could you give me examples of what you mean by contradictions?" Believe it or not, most of the time, they cannot produce a single one. But that doesn't get you off the hook–you still need to be ready to give a defense of what you believe and why you believe it (1 Peter 3:15). Now, what if they produce what *they* believe are legitimate contradictions in the Gospels (or other parts of the Bible for that matter)? How do you respond?

This question can be answered quite easily with a little common sense, honest investigation of the Scripture, and the application of a method called SiMPLe C. After showing you this very effective approach to addressing alleged contradictions, we will use parts of this method to "debunk" two that are commonly referred to. Finally, we will look at how God's character is the standard for what we can expect to see in His Word.

SiMPLe C: Know it!

(**Note**: This method is introduced in one of our DeBunked videos, "The Bible Is Full of Errors," available on our Reasons for Hope app, along with hundreds of other resources free of charge.)

S–Spelling

M–Mistranslation

P–Perspective

L–Literal vs. Figurative

C–Context

S–Spelling:

Many so-called errors are simply variants in spelling; for example, a word translated from Greek into old English might have a different spelling than American English. British translators would write *theatre* ending in "-re," and Americans would write *theater* ending in "-er." That's not an error; it's a variation in spelling.

M–Mistranslation:

What some might call a mistranslation is simply a case where the original word might not have an exact equivalent in the translated language. For instance, there are multiple Greek words for love, with meaning that range from erotic to platonic, but only one in English. Context and comparison can easily solve the differences.

P–Perspective:

The Bible was inspired by the Holy Spirit and penned by more than forty authors. What skeptics often refer to as different accounts of the same event are actually just different perspectives, as in the four gospels (Matthew, Mark, Luke, and John respectively), which present the life and ministry of Christ as: 1) the coming Messiah; 2) the suffering Servant; 3) the Son of Man; and 4) the Son of God. The focus of each of the authors varies. Quite often, authors recounting the same event will provide additional details. These basic differences, like reading about someone named John Smith as a father in one book and as a husband in another, actually show that the writers worked independently of each other and did not collaborate on their accounts.[68]

---

[68]Jay Seegert, *Creation & Evolution: Compatible or In Conflict?* (Green Forest, AR: Master Books, 2014), 163-164.

In his book, *Forensic Faith*, J. Warner Wallace further elaborates on the credibility of the gospels based on the eyewitness perspective of the writers.[69]

> Evidence mattered to the earliest believers. They trusted the accounts offered by John and Matthew because these men knew Jesus personally. These disciples provided direct evidence in their gospels. Luke's gospel was embraced by the early church on the basis of Luke's evidential, investigative approach. Luke interviewed the eyewitnesses and included their testimony. Even Mark's gospel was accepted based on its eyewitness value. While Mark may not have known Jesus personally, his gospel, according to the first-century bishop Papias of Hierapolis, was the accurate collection of testimony from an important eyewitness, Simon Peter.[70]

L–Literal vs. Figurative:

God's Word contains many writing styles (poetry, song, narrative) and also figurative language (similes, metaphors, analogies). To accurately interpret the Bible, we must understand both the writing style and the use of figurative language; for example, Jesus referred to Himself using figurative language: the Door, the Bread, the Vine, the Light, the Lamb, the Stone, the Shepherd, and more. By looking at the immediate context, using common sense, and comparing it with the rest of Scripture, we understand that when Jesus says He's the Door, He doesn't mean He's a wooden rectangle that swings on hinges.

C–Context:

Most alleged error issues arise when people don't acknowledge the proper context of a verse, quote only part of it, or purposefully misuse it. For instance, they might argue that John 3:16 says, "For God so loved..." but Deuteronomy 16:22 says: "...the Lord your God hates." This is an absurd comparison, because the context of John 3:16 is about

[69]J. Warner Wallace, *Forensic Faith* (Colorado Springs, CO: David C. Cook, 2017), 52.

[70]Papias said the following about Mark's relationship to Peter: "Mark, having become the interpreter of Peter, wrote down accurately, though not indeed in order, whatsoever he remembered of the things said or done by Christ." Papias, quoted in Eusebius, "Church History," *Nicene and Post-Nicene Fathers,* eds. Philip Schaff and Henry Wallace (New York: Cosimo, 2007), 172.

God's love for people, and the Deuteronomy verse is talking about His hate for altars to foreign gods. Without a heart for truth, people can pretty much claim the Bible says anything they want if they take it out of context.

The phrase "context is king" means that context is crucial to biblical understanding, which will resolve most alleged errors. Always read what comes before and after a particular verse or passage. Reading the passage, the chapter, or even the entire book will give you a better understanding and application of the verse in question. It's also important to understand that *context* encompasses four principles:

1) **Content**–Literally, what does it say?
2) **History**–Where, when, and to whom were the words spoken, and how was it understood at that time? It is of great importance to note that "archaeology has repeatedly verified many events and locations found in the Bible, giving an ever-growing confidence in the accuracy and inspiration of God's Word."[71]
3) **Grammar**–The immediate sentence or passage and the way in which it is presented (i.e., literal versus figurative language).
4) **Synthesis**–Cross-referencing with other verses in Scripture (Always consider context when cross-referencing. Although you may find the same word, the context can affect its meaning.)

TWO "APPARENT" CONTRADICTIONS:

Some of the alleged contradictions in the Gospels focus on comparing what Jesus says and attempting to argue that He contradicts Himself. A typical example is found in the Gospel of John. Consider the following two verses:

1. "If I bear witness of Myself, **my witness is not true"** (John 5:31, emphasis added).
2. Jesus answered and said to them, "Even if I bear witness of Myself, **my witness is true**, for I know where I came from and where I am going; but you do not know where I come from and where I am going" (John 8:14, emphasis added).

[71]Seegert, *Creation & Evolution,* 165.

In the first verse, Jesus says that if He bears witness of Himself, it's not true, but three chapters later, He claims that if He bears witness of Himself, it is true. Isn't that a contradiction? No.

To properly understand the first reference *in its context* (literal and historical), we need to read the verses immediately surrounding it. It's clear that when Jesus speaks here, He is responding to their twisted perspective on His nature. Let's paraphrase what Jesus said like this: ***"Since you consider Me to be only a human, my testimony of Myself isn't valid in your eyes. So, since that's not good enough for you, I've got another witness that testifies for Me too."***

Again, with the second verse, to get the context, we need to consider the surrounding verses. Here Jesus is answering the same question asked by a Pharisee, but this time He answers the question by referencing His true nature: ***"Even if I testify of Myself and this is all you had, My testimony is valid because I am one with the Father, who sent Me."*** In other words, if Jesus was only a man, His testimony could be untrue at times. But, since He was God manifest in the flesh, His testimony is true **all the time**. Context definitely makes things clearer, and in this case, it helps us dismiss the supposed "contradiction" as unsustainable.

Another common approach is to juxtapose two passages from different parts of the Bible to highlight a supposed contradiction. Consider the following two passages.

1. "Peace I leave with you, my peace I give to you; not as the world gives do I give to you. Let not your heart be troubled, neither let it be afraid" (John 14:27).
2. "Do not think that I came to bring peace on Earth. I did not come to bring peace but a sword" (Matthew 10:34).

The key to unpacking this supposed contradiction is to ask ourselves who Jesus is talking to (the history and synthesis of the context). In John 14:27, the answer is simple: He is addressing the disciples. He has been speaking to them since the beginning of chapter 13 and does not conclude this speech until the end of chapter 17. These are Jesus' final words to His disciples prior to His arrest and crucifixion and are meant to bring them comfort. Here he shows them that the ultimate end of the Gospel is peace with God.

However, in Matthew 10:34, Jesus–also speaking to His disciples– was showing that the *immediate* result of the Gospel is often conflict. "Conversion to Christ can result in strained family relationships (Matthew 10:35,36), persecution, and even martyrdom. Following Christ presupposes a willingness to endure such hardships (Matthew 10:32,33; 10:37-39). Christ will have no one deluded into thinking that He calls believers to a life devoid of all conflict."[72] We also have to keep in mind the word *"peace"* is used differently in both passages. In John, He is extending internal peace—peace of mind and of spirit, that their hearts may not be troubled. In Matthew, Jesus is speaking of political/ cultural peace. Jesus was letting His disciples know that they would not be exempt from experiencing future troubles, but they would have His supernatural peace to sustain them.

WHAT GOD SAYS ABOUT THE ACCURACY OF HIS WORD

God claims that His Word is inspired, which in the Greek means that He breathed it out Himself (2 Timothy 3:16). You might be asking, "But wasn't it men who wrote the Bible?" Yes, but these men were chosen by God, and they wrote what the Holy Spirit (God Himself) moved them to write as stated in 2 Peter 1:19-21: "And so we have the prophetic word confirmed, which you do well to heed as a light that shines in a dark place, until the day dawns and the morning star rises in your hearts; knowing this first, that no prophecy of Scripture is of any private interpretation, **for prophecy never came by the will of man, but holy men of God spoke as they were moved by the Holy Spirit"** (emphasis added).

This passage is saying that no person can understand the truths of the Bible without God revealing these truths to them. In fact, the Apostle Paul, who wrote at least thirteen of the twenty-seven New Testament books, mentions this three different times (1 Corinthians 2:13-14; 1 Corinthians 14:37; and 1 Thessalonians 2:13).

So, although men were the *means* by which God wrote the Bible, and we know men can make mistakes, God specifically states that *He* never

---

[72]John MacArthur, *The MacArthur Study Bible (ESV)* (Nashville: Thomas Nelson, 2021), 1282.

makes mistakes. Therefore, if God is the One who is directing what these men were to write, would He not guard against errors and contradictions?

GOD IS UNABLE TO CONTRADICT HIMSELF

Remember, God is always true (Romans 3:3-4; Jeremiah 10:10; John 1:14; 14:6; 17:3). Because of that, He cannot not lie (Numbers 23:19; 1 Samuel 15:29; and Titus 1:1-3). This is why the Bible puts so much emphasis on the fact that it is true from beginning to end (John 17:14-17; Psalm 119:142,151,160; Revelation 21:5; 22:6). The fact is, either man or God must be the authority defining what is truthful and trustworthy and what is not. In accordance with the very nature of God, we would have to come to the logical conclusion that *He* is that Authority, and therefore His Word is the standard against which all truth must be measured.

CONCLUSION

As we looked at these apparent "contradictions" in the gospels, we can see that they could be answered quite simply using the SiMPLe C method and trusting the authenticity and authority of God and His Word. Indeed, "Let God be true though everyone were a liar, as it is written, 'That you may be justified in your words, and prevail when you are judged'" (Romans 3:4).

You have no reason to fear trusting in God's Word. We encourage you not to stop here; do some more digging. To go deeper into this topic or apologetics in general, may I suggest you read the following resources:

- *Keeping Faith in an Age of Reason* by Dr. Jason Lisle
- *Demolishing Supposed Bible Contradictions ... Volume 1 & 2* edited by Ken Ham.
- *Creation & Evolution: Compatible or In Conflict?* by Jay Seegert
- *Forensic Faith* by J. Warner Wallace
- *Tactics* by Greg Koukl

Chapter 23

HOW DO WE KNOW THE BIBLE HASN'T CHANGED LIKE THE TELEPHONE GAME?

Dave Glander

(The New Testament section was written by Hannah Dukes.)

Let's face it, when your turn comes while playing the game of telephone, don't you try to butcher what the last person said, just to make it that much funnier? Of course, you do! The whole point of the game is to see just how ridiculous the change *is* between what the original statement was and what the last person hears.

However, there is a massive difference between the objectives in the game of telephone and how God's written Word has come down to us. The game's outright intention is to get it wrong. This approach is directly opposite of the diligent, meticulous effort made throughout the centuries to maintain the authenticity of the Old and New Testaments.

THE WHOLE TRUTH AND NOTHING BUT THE TRUTH, SO HELP US GOD.

To begin, let's examine the makeup of what is known as the Holy Bible. The Bible consists of a total of sixty-six books divided into two sections: The first thirty-nine of these books comprise the Old Testament (OT), and the remaining twenty-seven books make up the New Testament (NT). Questions about the inerrancy (complete accuracy) of the Bible are focused mainly on the NT. However, it is profoundly important that we also confirm the reliability of the OT, as it contains vital information about subjects such as the following: creation, original sin, the foundation of the family unit, ways to live in God's perfect will, and over 350 prophecies[73] about the arrival of Jesus Christ–the overall theme of the entire sixty-six books from Genesis to Revelation.

THE OLD TESTAMENT

To become a board-certified medical doctor (MD), you must complete a four-year undergraduate program, attend medical school for another four years, then enroll for a three-year residential program. Only then can you finally take a licensing exam to start your career as a doctor! If you graduate from high school at the age of eighteen, you'll be twenty-nine years old before you start making money as an MD.

Phew … I'm exhausted just thinking about that!

Likewise, there was a rigorous, three-level, educational process in place before and during the time of Jesus to become a scribe. Most Jewish scribes responsible for making copies of OT scrolls didn't start their careers until at least the age of thirty![74]

Level 1: Bet Sefer (House of the Book)

Many scholars believe that both girls and boys from age five to twelve years old would attend Bet Sefer to learn to read and write, while also memorizing and studying the Torah, the first five books

---

[73]"351 Old Testament Prophecies Fulfilled in Jesus Christ," *New Testament Christians.com* (n.d.). https://www.newtestamentchristians.com/bible-study-resources/351-old-testament-prophecies-fulfilled-in jesus-christ/

[74]Ray Vander Laan, "Rabbi and Talmidim," *That the World May Know* (Updated 2021). Accessed December 13, 2021. https://www.thattheworldmayknow.com/rabbi-and-talmidim. See also https://sefaria.org/Pirkei_Avot.5.21?lang=bi

of the OT.[75]

Level 2: Bet Midrash (House of Study)

Only boys would progress to the second level, spending the next two to three years in a more intense study of the Torah, and learning to apply it to specific situations. Most of them would also be learning a trade during this time as well.

Level 3: Bet Talmud (House of Learning)[76]

At this point, the truly gifted would have proven their ability to memorize the complete Torah. They could state a position and defend it by cross-referencing passages to show their understanding of the Law. A rabbi would select and carefully train these gifted ones, a process that was lengthy and intensive, lasting from the age of fifteen to thirty.[77]

Compare the discipline of these young men with a modern-day example of my friend, Chris, who was born blind. When around her, I noticed that anytime a Bible verse was mentioned, her husband would ask her where the verse was located. Chris, without exception, "rattled off" the reference, and often added in cross-references for the same topic. One day, I had to ask if she had the entire Bible memorized. She answered yes, because a braille Bible consists of an entire series of twenty-seven enormous braille books. Taking these to church would require a wheelbarrow! Chris said that it just became easier for her to memorize each passage so that when the pastor said to turn to a location in the Bible, she could do so in her mind.

These examples shed light on how difficult it would have been for any part of the OT to have been intentionally and significantly changed. To successfully alter any of the OT writings, it would have been necessary to erase the memories of tens of thousands of people who had retained the holy words their forefathers had meticulously passed down to them.[78] If someone had attempted to change anything,

---

[75]"Bet Sefer: Covered in the Dust of Your Rabbi," *Wordpress* (n.d.). https://coveredinthedustoftherabbi. wordpress.com/about/bet-sefer/

[76]Dan Stolebarger, "Discipleship vs. Talmidim," *Koinonia House*, November 1, 2005. https://www.khouse.org/articles/2005/616

[77]Ray Vander Laan, "Synagogue School," *That the World May Know* (Updated 2021). https://www.thattheworldmayknow.com/synagogue-school

[78]Vander Laan, "Rabbi and Talmidim." https://www.thattheworldmayknow.com/rabbi-and-talmidim

someone else would have immediately corrected them. As a matter of fact, many people within earshot would have rebuked the speaker for *anything* he said in error. Try to play the game of telephone that way… boy, what a boring game that would be!

GOING FROM VOICE TO TEXT TRANSMISSION

Let's now move from the verbal transmission of holy writings to the actual process of making a written copy of them. Any high schooler can tell you that writing an essay for a class project can take a very long time and be quite the undertaking. How would you feel if you submitted your completed 2,500-word essay to your teacher and had it returned to you marked "unacceptable" because it had one–just one–spelling error? What does your teacher expect, perfection? Yet, that's *exactly* what would happen to a scribe's work if he made one single error in his copying.

Meticulous requirements were in place to ensure that every copy was accurate. In fact, the Hebrew word for scribe was "sofer," meaning "one who counts letters." A scribe would literally count every single letter in both the original manuscript and the copy he was making to ensure they matched perfectly. If the numbered letters didn't match perfectly, that meant there was an error somewhere.[79] At that point, the scribe could not continue working on the project until the mistake was found, properly corrected, and proofread again. These steps, plus many more, were effective in guarding against error, and modern archeology confirms how trustworthy our copies are.

A BOY – A ROCK – A HOLE – AND A TIMELESS TREASURE!

In early spring of 1947, a Bedouin boy named Muhammed was tending to his sheep near the western shore of the Dead Sea. He tossed a rock into a hole in a cave and to his surprise, heard something break. Investigating, he found multiple tall clay jars filled with some of the most ancient manuscripts ever discovered. Along with many other historical writings was a copy of *every single book* in the Hebrew Bible, except for Esther. The cave's climate had preserved these 2,000-year-old pieces of parchment and papyrus.

---

[79]Josh McDowell, "Meticulous Scribe, Trusted Manuscript," *Josh McDowell Ministry* (January 7, 2019). https://www.josh.org/meticulous-scribes-trusted-manuscript/

One of the scrolls contained the entire Book of Isaiah, dated to around 125-100 BC. Because the incredibly precise prophecies in Isaiah 53 were perfectly fulfilled at Jesus's death, some have wondered if that chapter was truly authentic. Had it been changed (telephone-game-style) to reflect the historical narratives of the early church? Let's review the prophecies in question:

- "He was despised and rejected by men."
- "Surely He has borne our griefs and carried our sorrows; yet we esteemed Him stricken, smitten by God, and afflicted."
- "He was wounded for our transgressions, He was bruised for our iniquities; The chastisement for our peace was upon Him, And by His stripes we are healed."
- "And the Lord has laid on Him the iniquity of us all."
- "He had done no violence, nor was any deceit in His mouth."
- "Yet it pleased the Lord to bruise Him; He has put Him to grief. When You make His soul an offering for sin."
- "By His knowledge My righteous Servant shall justify many, for He shall bear their iniquities."
- "He poured out His soul unto death, and He was numbered with the transgressors, and He bore the sin of many, and made intercession for the transgressors."

With the 1947 discovery of the Isaiah scroll that predated the historical event of Jesus's death by over one hundred years, it became obvious that Isaiah 53 had not been modified by Christians. The Dead Sea Scrolls took the date of the earliest known copies of Isaiah back nearly 1000 years and revealed that the text had been transmitted accurately through the years![80]

THE NEW TESTAMENT

For many years, scholars have investigated whether the New Testament we have today is the same as the original authors' manuscripts. Naturally, this short response will not go to that same depth, but we *will*

[80]Clarence L. Haynes, Jr., "What Every Christian Should Know about the Dead Sea Scrolls," *Bible Study Tools* (March 25, 2021). https://www.biblestudytools.com/bible-study/topical-studies/what-every-christian-should-know-about-the-dead-sea-scrolls.html

address some key facts.

To date, there are more than 20,000 manuscripts[81] of New Testament writings in various languages (including Greek and Latin) that have been carefully catalogued, studied, and compared. Within these copies, there are 300,000-400,000 documented variants.[82] This immense number might seem imposing until we realize, "A textual variant is *any place among the [manuscripts] in which there is variation in wording, including word order, omission, or addition of words, even spelling differences.* The most trivial changes count, and even when all the manuscripts except one say the same thing, that lone [manuscript's] reading counts as a textual variant."[83] (emphasis in original) Daniel B. Wallace, one of the most respected New Testament textual scholars of our day, states, "The reason we have a lot of variants is that we have a lot of manuscripts… (T)o speak about the number of variants without also speaking about the number of manuscripts is simply an appeal to sensationalism."[84] These differences affect *no essential tenet* of the Christian faith.[85]

Bart Ehrman, author of *Misquoting Jesus,* as well as other provocatively titled works, is also a world-recognized New Testament textual scholar. However, he has been a leader in the attack *against* the reliability of the New Testament manuscripts. When speaking or writing to the non-academic world, he tends to focus on the most drastic variants, giving the false impression that he is exposing one of many known significant changes. He claims that:

- The original manuscripts have been copied … and copied … and copied (like the telephone game), and the copies we

---

[81]"The Manuscripts," *Institute for Creation Research*. Accessed December 14, 2021. https://www.icr.org/bible-manuscripts

[82]Daniel Wallace, "The Number of Textual Variants: An Evangelical Miscalculation," *Daniel B. Wallace* (September 9, 2013). https://danielbwallace.com/2013/09/09/the-number-of-textual-variants-an-evangelical-miscalculation/

[83]Daniel B. Wallace, *Revisiting the Corruption of the New Testament* (Grand Rapids, MI: Kregel Academic, 2011), 26.

[84]Ibid.

[85]Daniel Wallace, "Five More Myths about Bible Translations and the Transmission of the Text," *Daniel B. Wallace* (December 28, 2012). See especially under "Myth 4." https://danielbwallace.com/2012/12/28/five-more-myths-about-bible-translations-and-the-transmission-of-the-text

have contain so many differences, we cannot possibly know what the original text was.[86]

- Most likely, the scribes were *intentional* in their corruption of the text.[87]

The last point is fascinating, considering that he also claims it can't be known what the original said, so how can it be claimed that it was corrupted?

Interestingly enough, when he speaks to the academic world, he is not nearly so assertive that the catalogued changes are as critical as he makes them out to be in other settings. Could it be he is well aware that his claims could not hold up under the scrutiny of other textual scholars? It would seem so, and the truth is, *the NT is by far the best-attested work from the ancient world.*[88] Ehrman himself admits, in the appendix to Misquoting Jesus (paperback edition), that "Essential Christian beliefs are not affected by textual variants in the manuscript tradition of the New Testament."[89]

Wallace also addresses our topic question directly in his book when he says, "The impression that many readers get from *Misquoting Jesus* is that the transmission of the NT resembles the 'telephone game.' As the tale goes from person to person, it gets terribly garbled. The whole point of the telephone game, in fact, is to see how garbled it can get. *There is no motivation to 'get it right.'* By the time it gets to the last person, who repeats it aloud for the whole group, everyone has a good laugh. But the copying of NT manuscripts is hardly like this parlor game, for many reasons.

1. The message is passed on in writing, not orally. Passing a message in writing would make for a pretty boring telephone game!
2. Rather than having one line, there are *multiple* lines or streams of transmission.

[86]Bart D. Ehrman, *Misquoting Jesus* (New York: Harper Collins, 2005), 10.

[87]Ibid., 53.

[88]Tim Chaffey, "Can We Trust the New Testament Manuscripts?" *Ark Encounter* (Updated 2021). https://arkencounter.com/bible-true/beans/

[89]Ehrman, *Misquoting Jesus*, 252.

3. Textual critics do not rely on just the last person in each line but can interrogate several folks who are closer to the original source.
4. Patristic writers [i.e., church fathers] are commenting on the text as it is going through its transmissional history. And when there are chronological gaps among the manuscripts, these writers often fill in those gaps by telling us what the text said in that place in their day.
5. In the telephone game, once the story is told by one person, that individual has nothing else to do with the story. It is out of his or her hands. But the original NT books were most likely copied more than once and may have been consulted even after a few generations of copies had been produced."[90] (emphasis in original)

IF THE BIBLE CAN'T BE CONSIDERED ACCURATE HISTORY, NOTHING CAN!

If we compare the manuscript evidence we have for other ancient documents, none of them comes even close to the number of copies that we currently have for the NT! The closest runner up is Homer's *Iliad* with fewer than 2,000 copies, and many of these have major differences in the details of events. Even more poorly represented are the combined works for Alexander the Great, Aristotle, Julius Caesar, etc. But here's the thing: *Nobody* questions the authenticity or reliability of any of these works of ancient history. If the NT were judged in the same manner as these works, it would "blow them out of the water"! As a matter of fact, if the standard of accuracy for all ancient historical documents were set by the NT, then these other words of ancient history would have to be thrown out, because none of them come up to the level of authenticity and viability of the NT. The famous British manuscript expert, Sir Frederick Kenyon, summed up the matter well when he declared that:

> The interval between the dates of original composition and the earliest extant evidence becomes so small as to be in fact negligible, and **the last foundation for any doubt that the**

[90]Wallace, "The Number of Textual Variants ..." https://danielbwallace.com/2013/09/09/the-number-of-textual-variants-an-evangelical-miscalculation/

> **Scriptures have come down substantially as they were written has now been removed.** Both the authenticity and the general integrity of the books of the New Testament may be regarded as finally established.[91] (emphasis added)

CONCLUSION

The Bible is the only book in the world that has held up under the intense scrutiny of its authenticity. The vast number of prophecies found in the OT that are fulfilled in the NT are unprecedented. There is no way an author could predict a future occurrence without the divine knowledge of the One True God who inspired the author to write. The Bible tells us that "prophecy never came by the will of man, but holy men of God spoke as they were moved by the Holy Spirit" (2 Peter 1:21), and that "all Scripture is given by inspiration of God…" (2 Timothy 3:16).

So, the real question is this: If the Bible really is the written Word of God, then wouldn't that same God who inspired the writers of His Word also PRESERVE His Word throughout the ages? Even Jesus tells us in Matthew 5:18 (NIV), "For truly I tell you, until heaven and earth disappear, not the smallest letter, not the least stroke of a pen, will by any means disappear from the Law until everything is accomplished."

God is the ultimate author of the Bible. But equally important to us is that He has protected His Word and has confirmed in His Word that "the living and abiding Word of God . . . remains forever" (1 Peter 1:23b, 25a)! "For the word of God is living and active, and sharper than any two-edged sword, even penetrating as far as the division of soul and spirit" (Hebrews 4:12, NASB).

[91]Frederic Kenyon, *The Bible and Archaeology* (London: George G. Harrap & Co., 1940), 288.

Chapter 24

HOW CAN YOU USE THE BIBLE TO PROVE THE BIBLE? THAT DOESN'T MAKE SENSE!

JUAN VALDES

The person asking this question believes the common misconception that if we as Christians use one portion of the Bible to "prove" or argue in favor of the truthfulness of another portion, we're engaging in circular reasoning.

In their book, *A Workbook for Arguments: A Complete Course in Critical Thinking (Indianapolis: Hackett Publishing Company, 2011),* David R. Morrow and Anthony Weston define circular reasoning as "implicitly using your conclusion as a premise ... the argument assumes just what it is trying to prove."

To address this question, we must consider two things:

- What is meant by "prove the Bible"?
- What are examples of both appropriate and inappropriate uses of the Bible when presenting a defense of the Truth?

WHAT IS CIRCULAR REASONING?

As we see on the previous page, circular reasoning is a way of arguing where we reach a conclusion that is supported by a premise that itself is supported by the conclusion. Something like: A is true because of B, which itself is true because of A, which is true because of B, which is true because of A, *ad infinitum*. It can also be called "begging the question." Unless we bring in outside information in support of our conclusion, we can't escape the circularity of the argument. For example, "Drinking and driving is wrong because driving under the influence of alcohol is illegal." Notice that both the premise and the conclusion are true. However, it's not a very good argument. The conclusion simply repeats the supporting premise using a synonymous phrase. The phrases "is wrong" and "is illegal" say the same thing; no new information has been added.

To escape the circularity, additional support must be added to back the idea that it's the "wrong" thing to do. This can be done in several ways. For example, we can appeal to the scientific data proving that alcohol in the bloodstream slows reaction time, affects your motor skills (such as eye, hand, and foot coordination), reduces concentration, and decreases vision–all of which can lead to an accident. These facts help support *why* it's the wrong thing to do. Another supporting argument could focus on the statistics of people killed by drunk drivers, establishing it as a morally wrong thing to do. It's important to note that just because a circular argument has been used doesn't mean that the premises or the conclusion are necessarily false; it simply means that we've not proven our point. Speaking of points, what is the point of trying to "prove the Bible?"

WHAT DOES IT MEAN TO "PROVE" THE BIBLE?

A phrase like "proving the Bible" can have more than one meaning. It is important to know exactly what we are trying to "prove," because *how* we go about "proving" something depends on *what* we are trying to prove. In dealing with contemporary atheists and agnostics, it is common for this idea of proving the Bible to mean one of four things. First, it could be referring to proving that the Bible *is trustworthy*. Second, it could mean proving the Bible *is authentic*. Third, it could mean proving that the Bible *is the Word of God*. Finally, it could mean proving that *a specific event* recorded in the Bible did in fact happen. Let's take a brief look at these.

- ***What would it take to prove that the Bible is trustworthy?*** When we speak of the trustworthiness of the Bible, we're referring to the truthfulness of its content. When the Bible says something, can we believe it? Proving the trustworthiness of the Bible can be done in numerous ways, depending on what type of content is being evaluated for its truthfulness.

  For example, if we want to prove the historical accuracy of the Bible's content, a strong evidential case can be made based on modern archaeology. Archaeological discoveries continue to confirm the content of the Bible. Quite often we learn that a fact once questioned due to lack of evidence has now been proven to be true by the latest evidence uncovered.

- ***What would it take to prove that the Bible is authentic?*** When we question the authenticity of the Bible, we are questioning whether the Bible we have today is anything like the original manuscripts (also called autographs). Has it been corrupted? Has it changed over the years? These are valid questions that must be addressed. Fortunately, the Bible has undergone the harshest scrutiny of any ancient manuscript ever.[92] Every variation in every known copy of the New Testament spanning almost two thousand years of copying has been documented. Anyone with knowledge of the original Greek language can purchase the latest edition of the Greek New Testament edited by Nestle-Aland and see extensive documenting of the variations.

  What's the result of all this scrutiny? The authenticity of the New Testament is established beyond a reasonable doubt. Regarding the Old Testament, the discovery of

---

[92]See the chapter entitled, "How Do We Know the Bible Hasn't Changed Like the Telephone Game?" for more detail.

the Dead Sea scrolls in the late 1940s allowed us to compare entire books in our modern translations (i.e., Isaiah) with the oldest copies of these books ever found. Again, the text we have proved to be practically exact to that of the ancient texts. Much more could be added, but argumentation along these lines goes a long way in establishing the biblical text as authentic.

- ***What would it take to prove that the Bible is God's Word?*** The easiest way to prove that the Bible is God's Word is to provide evidence of content that cannot be of human origin. The most straightforward way is to consider fulfilled prophecies. Humans cannot accurately predict the future at the detailed levels we find in the Bible. Sure, we can predict that it will rain someday in the future, and we will be proven right. But this is not the kind of prediction we find in the Bible.

  The Old Testament prophets predicted incredibly precise details regarding the coming Messiah that ALL came true with astonishing accuracy. For example, it was predicted that the Messiah would be betrayed for 30 pieces of silver (Zechariah 11:12,13; Matthew 27:9,10). Not 29 or 31 pieces; not gold coins, copper coins, or bronze coins; it had to be exactly 30 pieces of silver. Furthermore, this was predicted hundreds of years before it happened. There are close to 100 more examples of prophecies like this.[93] For those that are seeking the truth, this type of evidence is compelling.

- ***What would it take to prove that a particular event in the Bible did occur?*** I believe this is where we as Christians are often accused of using circular reasoning. How do we know that Jesus rose from the dead? One way to establish this, and many other events in the Bible, is to find corroborating witnesses in other portions of the Bible. One could argue that if Matthew, Mark,

[93] J. Barton Payne, *Encyclopedia of Biblical Prophecy: The Complete Guide to Scriptural Predictions and Their Fulfillment* (Eugene, OR: Wipf and Stock, 2020), 147.

> Luke, John, Peter, and Paul all affirm the resurrection of Jesus—as eyewitnesses—it is a well-documented event. This is where antagonists go nuts. "Isn't it circular reasoning to use the Bible to prove that something in the Bible is true?!" NO. Not in the way I argue above. Let me explain: The misconception occurs because people speak of the Bible as if it were one source, but it isn't.

The Bible is a collection of sixty-six different books, written at different times, by at least forty different human authors. If I use Matthew's Gospel to verify something in John's Gospel, it is not circular reasoning. I am appealing to an independent source (Matthew) to verify another independent source (John). It's a perfectly legitimate way of verifying historical events. Furthermore, nobody denies that the books of the Bible are authentic ancient documents. Their testimony cannot be dismissed, unless there's specific evidence that disqualifies the specific documents alluded to. This is no different than verifying the identity of a criminal by calling several eyewitnesses to the stand who can identify him as the person they saw committing the crime. Once we understand that the Bible is a collection of books (written by independent sources), this type of accusation of circular reasoning collapses.

WHEN IS IT APPROPRIATE TO USE THE BIBLE IN PRESENTING A DEFENSE OF THE TRUTH?

Sometimes, however, Christians do engage in circular reasoning. For example, I've often heard people say that "the Bible is the Word of God." No problem there. I believe that is absolutely true. But in the defense of that claim, things tend to get circular very fast. When asked how they know that to be the case, they respond, "because God says so." That response (in and of itself) is not irrational or illogical. I believe that's absolutely true as well. But when challenged further as to where God says this, they respond "in the Bible." This is *not* a good argument, instead, it's a textbook example of circular reasoning, which Christians

> *Our responsibility is to present solid, rational, valid reasons in support of what we believe.*

should avoid. Appealing to the Bible as evidence can be done, but it must be done legitimately, as we discussed in the previous section.

CONCLUSION

Before attempting to present arguments in favor of any conclusion, it's wise to ask those we're trying to persuade exactly what they would consider enough evidence. It's quite common to present an excellent argument to prove a point only to find that the goal post has been moved. One may discover a bit too late–for example, after presenting numerous arguments in favor of the divine authorship of the Bible–that nothing we could possibly say would ever be enough to persuade the individual we're engaging with. Some people refuse to believe, regardless of the evidence presented. Our responsibility is to present solid, rational, valid reasons in support of what we believe. Our faith is not blind; there is ample evidence that supports it. However, we cannot control the beliefs of others. At the end of the day, everyone must make a choice to either believe it or not.

PART FIVE

THE CHARACTER OF GOD

Chapter 25

WHY DOESN'T GOD MAKE HIMSELF MORE OBVIOUS? IT REALLY SEEMS LIKE HE'S NOT EVEN THERE.

Brian Scoggin

This question is arguably one of the most important questions that has ever been asked–not because of the question itself, but because the correct answer to this question reveals why we live in a world filled with sin and death, and why God's judgment on this world is inevitable. It's so vital, in fact, that the Apostle Paul began his longest (and perhaps, his most important) letter, the book of Romans, by answering THIS question. He wrote: "For the wrath of God is being revealed from heaven against all ungodliness and unrighteousness of men, who by their unrighteousness suppress the **TRUTH. For what can be known about God is plain to them, because God has shown it to them**... **So, they are without excuse**" (Romans 1:18-19,20b, emphasis added).

WOW! There you have it: The Bible is clear about the question. God doesn't make Himself **more** obvious because, according to the Scriptures, He has made Himself **completely** obvious! As for sin, death, and judgment, this verse makes clear that all of it exists because people have a sin condition that makes it hard to recognize God for who He truly is, and this greatly affects how we live our lives. Now that we know this, let's look at the reasons why we may be missing Him.

"IF IT WERE A SNAKE, IT WOULD'VE BIT YA'!"

Have you heard this saying before? You might say it to someone who is having trouble finding an object that is sitting plainly within their reach. The Bible describes God as being this close to us and even takes it a step further. When Paul shared with the Athenian Greeks at the Areopagus, he described God as being not only near to us, but as the One in whom we exist. He says it like this, "Yet he (God) is not actually far from each one of us, for **'In him we live and move and have our being**'" (Acts 17:27b-28a, emphasis mine).

When it comes to us seeing God, picture a time when you may have walked into a pantry full of food and said, "There's nothing to eat in here!" Or other times when you may have walked into a closet full of clothes and complained, "I have nothing to wear!" It's funny how easily we say there is "nothing" when there is obviously plenty. What we are actually saying is, "There's nothing here that I *WANT*." This seems to be the idea that the apostle Paul is getting at when he says that people "by their unrighteousness suppress the truth."

To "*suppress the truth,*" in this case, means that even though people can see clearly that there is a true Creator God who owns the Universe and everything in it, they refuse to acknowledge Him because they reject His ways. You may ask, "What are His ways?"

To put it plainly, God's ways don't center around the glory of people; they center around the glory of God (Jeremiah 30:32).

To put it plainly, God's ways don't center around the glory of people; they center around the glory of God (Jeremiah 30:32). God created people and planned for them to be most fulfilled when He is at the very center of their lives. This is a problem for people born with a selfish nature that is opposed to giving God the glory that He alone deserves (Isaiah 43:7). Paul is helping the people to frame the problem correctly by essentially saying: "What can be known about God is obvious, but most people can't see Him because they are completely blinded by their own self-love, self-centeredness, and self-glorification!"

Paul goes on to explain that people have "exchanged the truth about God for a lie and worshiped the creature rather than the Creator…" (Romans 1:25). It's obvious that people naturally prefer themselves (or any other created thing they can see) as the object of their worship rather than an invisible Holy God with whom their sinful nature is at odds (Romans 5:12; 8:7-8; Isaiah 53:6; 1 John 1:8; Psalm 51:5).

Now we are beginning to identify the reason why we may feel that God is hard to perceive. According to God, He has made Himself completely obvious to everyone, so the problem with perceiving Him does not lie with God, but rather lies with us. Our prayer must become, "God, help me to see You because I know You're here."

WHAT'S SO OBVIOUS ABOUT GOD?

If we want to identify the things that should make God obvious to us, we'll need to start with some things we understand that can only be attributed to Him. So far, we've read that the Scriptures teach us that:

1. God has made Himself obvious to us all through the things that He has made.
2. The problem is not that He has not revealed Himself, but rather with our inability to recognize Him.

Again, Paul says it plainly in when he writes: "For [God's] invisible attributes, namely, his eternal power and divine nature, have been clearly perceived, ever since the creation of the world, in the things that have been made. So, they are without excuse" (Romans 1:20). We see in this verse that God is indeed invisible but has revealed Himself to us in the things that He has made.

Not only did God establish and create things that we can see, but He also claims responsibility for the existence of very real things that we cannot see, whether they are things in our *physical* world like wind or animal instincts, or things in the *metaphysical* world like the ability to feel emotion or the ability to reason. We can observe the EFFECTS of these things, but we cannot SEE the things themselves. God declares to us His power, nature, and existence in both things that are seen and things that are not seen (but are still very real). The question then becomes: Will we develop eyes to see God in all things?

TIME IS TICKIN' AWAY

In his letter to the Colossians, Paul spoke about God's power and glory in creation. He specifically referenced Jesus, God the Son, as Creator of everything we know. Paul says it like this: "For by him all things were created, in heaven and on earth, visible and invisible, whether thrones or dominions or rulers or authorities – all things were created through him and for him. He is before all things and in him all things hold together" (Colossians 1:16-17).

Paul confidently declares that God is responsible for everything that exists, whether visible or invisible, and therefore those things make Him extremely obvious to all who experience them. You may be asking, "How is God obvious through invisible things? Doesn't the fact that they are invisible make them not so obvious?" Not necessarily! Think about the concept of TIME for a second.

Unintentionally, I just used a measurement of time when I told you to think about time "for a second." Time is something that never stops affecting us. Not a second passes (See, there I go again!) without the reality of time affecting our mind and body. Let some time pass, and you'll get hungry, tired, older, etc. As you read this book, you might be thinking, "How *long* will this take?" or "*When* do I need to wrap this up?" We can't deny that time distinctly affects our everyday existence, and yet … you guessed it … it is INVISIBLE! This invisible reality that governs the welfare of our every breath and heartbeat began with God and exists within God because: "He is before all things and in him all things hold together" (Colossians 1:17). Time is just one of the many invisible things that God has created to display His power, nature, and glory to us.

In the same way, there are many things that God has created that are plain for us to see that should be attributed to Him as well. You see, God being Creator means that what He creates will forever belong to Him. They begin and end with Him. They are for His glory and our good. The Bible teaches us that: "by Him all things were created…" and "... in Him all things hold together." This means that all things belong to

God, and He has no plans to relinquish His authority over them. This is good news for us because we can't sustain them.

I remember when I came across the verses I began this chapter with (Romans 1:18-20). Paul's assertion that God should be so evident to us all was almost alarming to me. Paul went so far as to declare that "what can be known about God is plain to them, because God has shown it to them." I thought, "What is it that He has shown us that is so undeniably obvious?" I had always believed that it was a secret spiritual engagement that we entered into with God resulting in a confidence in God's existence. Although this is true to some degree (1 Corinthians 2:14), I was blown away to discover what God showed me as I wrestled with those verses that evening.

I was outdoors at a drive-in movie theater somewhere in rural Pennsylvania. It was a fall evening, and the leaves were all turning colors while the grass was still lush and green. The longing to understand how those verses could be true was weighing upon me. As I stood on the soft blanket of grass and looked around at God's creation around me, it was as if I heard Him suddenly whisper, "Do you see all this LIFE around you? I'm the only One who can do this." It hit me, "Oh my, yes!" My heart soared to Heaven in worship. I realized in that moment that everything around me and within me was surging with life. The grass was actively growing with life right under my feet! The trees were going through seasonal changes within their cycle of life. The birds were singing, the bugs were buzzing, and I was breathing and thinking.

As I stood on the soft blanket of grass and looked around at God's creation around me, it was as if I heard Him suddenly whisper, "Do you see all this LIFE around you? I'm the only One who can do this."

It all hit me so fast: God alone created life because God alone is life! He owns it and will never relinquish His authority over it. While we as human beings have become very smart, there are certain limitations that we will always have. There are things that we will never have the ability to create, things that God reserves for Himself and for His glory. Life is one of these things. In our scientific accomplishments, we have learned how to grow and manipulate life … but we cannot *create* it, and we never will, no matter how hard we try. This is reserved for God alone. We, as created beings, will never be able to truly create life.

CONCLUSION

Seeing it clearly

Now we hear the Apostle Paul's words ringing truer than ever to us when we read: "For although they knew God, they did not honor Him as God or give thanks to Him, but they became futile in their thinking, and their foolish hearts were darkened. Claiming to be wise, they became fools, and exchanged the glory of the immortal God for images resembling mortal man and birds and animals and creeping things" (Romans 1:21-23). God has given us wonderful things in rich abundance, but we rarely stop to honor Him and to show gratitude to Him. We all enjoy the wonderful things that God has so richly afforded us, while very rarely stopping to see Him and thank Him for them.

Our very lives, as well as the reality of every other visible and invisible thing, are due to God's existence.

Further on in Romans chapter 1, we read that many problems in our world result from people enjoying the amazing creation of God without giving Him the proper place of honor in their hearts for it. We've ignorantly credited ourselves, humanity, with the accomplishment of life and handled it wrongly, as if it's ours to do with as we please. Our very lives, as well as the reality of every other visible and invisible thing, are due to God's existence. We may ask, "*Why doesn't God make himself more obvious?*" Yet as we open our eyes to see God everywhere, the more fitting question is found in Psalm 139:7: *"Where can I go from Your Spirit, where can I flee from Your presence?"*

Chapter 26

I HAVE ASKED GOD PERSONALLY TO HELP MY EYESIGHT OR MY BIRTH DEFECT, AND HE HASN'T. WHY IS THAT?

Candace Nordine

Two years ago, I lost my dear friend, Katie, to cancer. She was a beautiful, young woman with a loving husband and five young daughters. Despite treatment, it was only a few short months from the time Katie was diagnosed to when she passed away. A heartbreaking twist to the story was that one of her daughters was adopted; she had lost her biological mother in Haiti, and now she had lost her adopted mother. Her friends and family had prayed continuously for Katie, with people praying for her each hour of the day and holding special prayer meetings just for her healing; it didn't make sense why God would take her life so soon.

Chances are that the question in this chapter is one we have all asked ourselves. It might not be cancer, eyesight, or a birth defect for you personally, but it's something. It all started back in the Garden of Eden when sin entered the world. The world which was once perfect was no longer perfect, and since then we have been feeling the effects that sin has on this world: death, disease, and pain.

GOD DOESN'T CHANGE—*JEHOVAH RAPHA*, OUR HEALER

God first declares Himself as *Jehovah Rapha*, the God-Who-Heals, in Exodus 15:26. The Israelites had fled from the Egyptians and were wandering in the wilderness. They finally found water, but it was bitter and undrinkable. Moses then prayed to God asking for provision.

There the Lord issued a ruling and instruction for them and put them to the test. He said, "If you listen carefully to the Lord your God and do what is right in his eyes, if you pay attention to his commands and keep all his decrees, I will not bring on you any of the diseases I brought on the Egyptians, for I am the Lord, who heals you (Exodus 15:25-26).

However, if God doesn't heal me or my loved one when I ask, does that mean God has changed and doesn't heal anymore? No, God healed then, and He can heal today. Scripture shows us that God does not change. Malachi 3:6 says, "For I the Lord do not change," and Hebrews 13:8 says, "Jesus Christ is the same yesterday and today and forever." In the Gospels, we see Jesus healing over and over again–does that hold any significance for us today? Let's look at three things we can learn from Jesus as He healed during His ministry on Earth.

1) Although God Can Heal Us, We Must Never Presume that He Must

In Luke 7:2, we read the account of a Roman centurion who sent some Jewish elders to Jesus because one of his highly valued servants was sick and about to die. The elders came to Jesus with the same attitude that we sometimes have about God healing us. They said, "He is worthy to have you do this for him" (Luke 7:4). Other translations use the words: "He deserves." That can often be our attitude when we ask God to heal us: "I am worthy, Lord. Surely I deserve this!"

Joni Eareckson Tada, a quadriplegic, probably knows more about this than most. At the age of 18, she was paralyzed from the shoulders down (a quadriplegic) after diving into a shallow pond. She writes:

> At first, I was troubled that God said "no" to my request [for healing]. But then I read an insightful passage in the Gospel of Mark. In the first chapter, Jesus is healing many sick people in Capernaum. The next day, the townspeople again brought their sick to Jesus early in the morning. Simon and his companions went to look for the Lord; "When they found him, they said, 'Everyone is looking for you.' But Jesus replied, 'We must go on to other towns as well, and I will preach to them, too. That is why I came.'" (Mark 1:38). It's not that Jesus did not care about the cancer-ridden or the paraplegics, it's just that their illnesses were not His main focus: the gospel was. Whenever people missed this–whenever they started coming to Him only to have their pains and problems removed—the Savior backed away.[94]

Joni discovered that day that Jesus' main purpose in coming was to heal hearts, not just our physical ailments. Eternity was (and is) at stake, and Jesus wants us to know that although He can heal us from our physical ailment, our ultimate reliance on Him for spiritual healing is far more important.

2) God's Ways Are Not Our Ways

"Now if we are children, then we are heirs—heirs of God and co-heirs with Christ, if indeed we share in his sufferings in order that we may also share in his glory" (Romans 8:17).

It's a hard concept to swallow, but God tells us over and over again that we will have suffering in this life, and that we should "count it all joy" (James 1:2). Sometimes that suffering will be a physical ailment. The comfort that we can have in this is that God has a plan and purpose for us even though we might not understand it.

The comfort that we can have in this is that God has a plan and purpose for us even though we might not understand it.

In John 11, two sisters named Mary and Martha summon Jesus. Their brother, Lazarus, had fallen ill and they knew Jesus

[94]Joni Earekson Tada, "Why Doesn't God Heal People We Love?" *Ann Voskamp* (December 2016). https://annvoskamp.com/2016/12/why-doesnt-god-heal-people-we-love/

could heal him. After all, they had sat under Jesus's teachings and heard His words. They were His friends. Surely, He would come for them–except He didn't. In fact, He waited two days before going to see them, and by that time Lazarus was dead. Mary confronted Jesus head-on: "Lord, if you had been here, my brother would not have died" (John 11:32). Although Jesus loved Mary and Martha (in fact, the Bible tells us He wept with them), He had a greater objective than simply healing a sick man. His intention was to raise Lazarus from the dead. In doing this, He demonstrated that He had power over death. Very shortly, He Himself would be killed, and the fact that He had resurrection power would mean more to the world than any other miracle. He was preparing to give them a reason for hope.

"I am the resurrection and the life. Whoever believes in me, though he die, yet shall he live, and everyone who lives and believes in me shall never die" (John 11:25). We are no different than Mary and Martha. All too often, we just want Jesus to show up when we ask and do what we ask, but we must remember that God's ways are higher than our ways and His thoughts higher than our thoughts (Isaiah 55:8-9).

3) God Sees Us Right Where We Are

Just because God doesn't seem to be healing you when you ask doesn't mean He doesn't see you or hear your prayers. If we read Luke 7, we see that Jesus raises a widow's son from the dead. Beyond the physical aspect of raising her son from the dead, we see that ultimately, He *saw* her and cared for her. "And when the Lord saw her, he had compassion on her and said to her, 'Do not weep'" (Luke 7:13). Jesus knew that the death of her son wouldn't just be a physical and emotional loss, but it would mean a life of poverty for this widow. She had lost her husband; now she had lost her son. She would have no one to support or care for her–Jesus saw her where she was at and had compassion.

God sees you, too. He knows just what you need when you need it.

As I write this, my father-in-law is battling cancer again. Shortly before they discovered the cancer had returned, he was in Thailand working with missionaries. This was right at the beginning of the

COVID-19 pandemic. Countries were shutting down and my in-laws decided they should leave the country earlier than they planned and get back to the United States. A week after they left, Thailand went on complete lockdown. Had they stayed, they would have been stuck in Thailand, probably for months. Within weeks of being back in the USA, they discovered the cancer had returned. Even before they saw their need to be back home, God saw.

God sees you, too. He knows just what you need when you need it. John Piper says, "God is always doing 10,000 things in your life, and you may be aware of three of them."[95]

My father-in-law recently shared this promise with our family from Psalm 13:5-6, "But I trust in your unfailing love, my heart rejoices in your salvation. I will sing the Lord's praise, for he has been good to me (NIV)." When it seems like God doesn't see you, trust in this promise. He loves you. He is for you. He sees you!

CONCLUSION

"I long to be with Christ ... because that is where the sting of death will be ultimately crushed. I want to stay on Earth and be with my family and enjoy this life, but it is amazing to know that this is as bad as it gets for me. I am temporarily stung by death, but as a believer, I will be united with Christ and those I have lost in death ... I long to be with Christ–it's better by far."

(Katie, 2008)

Katie wrote these words eleven years before the Lord took her home. Ultimately, she knew that sin, the deadly disease she needed healing from the most, was already taken care of when Jesus died for her on the cross. What an amazing reunion it will be some day to be with Katie again! If you know Christ, you also can look forward to a glorious reunion with Christ where there will be no more tears, no more sorrow, and we will have heavenly bodies free from the curse of sin!

---

[95]John Piper, "God Is Always Doing 10,000 Things in Your Life," *Desiring God* (January 1, 2013). https://www.desiringgod.org/articles/god-is-always-doing-10000-things-in-your-life

Chapter 27

IF JESUS WAS GOD, HOW COME HE DIDN'T KNOW WHEN HE WOULD RETURN?

Juan Valdes

God is difficult to understand. Though He has revealed Himself to us through the Bible, in the person of Jesus Christ, and through the natural world He created (Romans 1:20), there are still many mysteries that seem impenetrable from our limited human understanding. This shouldn't surprise us since the Creator of the entire universe and everything in it ought to be infinitely greater than us in *every* respect. That may have been what David was thinking when he burst out with the powerful words of Psalm 8, "When I look at your heavens, the work of your fingers, the moon and the stars, which you have set in place, what is man that you are mindful of him, and the son of man that you care for him?" (Psalm 8:3-4). Nevertheless, God has revealed Himself because He desires to be known (Jeremiah 9:24; Romans 1:19-20). Furthermore, God has given us a powerful mind with which to love Him (Matthew 22:37), and He encourages us to grow in our knowledge of Him.

Among the great mysteries surrounding God is the dual nature of Jesus. A clear example of the difficulty we encounter with the dual nature of Jesus is found in the Gospel of Matthew. When we consider Matthew 24:36, where Jesus tells the disciples that He doesn't know when the second coming will occur, we encounter an apparent contradiction. Many consider this as evidence that Jesus was merely human, not divine. After all, if there are things Jesus doesn't know, then He cannot be God, because God is supposed to know everything (Psalm 139:4; 147:5; 1 John 3:20). But if Jesus is God and knows everything, then He lied to the disciples—and God doesn't lie (Hebrews 6:18). This apparent contradiction brings to light a serious question: "Why were there things Jesus did not know?"

The key to understanding Jesus' limitations (despite His deity) is to consider the biblical teaching of His dual nature, so let's examine what the Bible says about that.

THE BIBLICAL CASE FOR JESUS' DUAL NATURE

Jesus was 100% human. There is a robust collection of biblical passages that emphasize His humanity. He was the natural born son of Mary. He was known as the son of a carpenter from Nazareth (although the Bible is clear that Joseph was not His biological father). Jesus possessed all essential elements of a human being. He had a soul (Mark 14:34), a body (John 19:38-40), and a spirit (John 13:21). He experienced basic human necessities such as hunger (Matthew 4:2), thirst (John 19:28), and exhaustion (Matthew 8:24). As a human being He learned, grew, worked, slept, ate, and prayed. The biblical case for Jesus' humanity is indisputable.

Jesus was 100% divine. There is also a robust collection of biblical passages that emphasize Jesus' deity. He was engaged in divine activities. He created the universe (John 1:1-3). He forgave sins (Matthew 9:1-8). He is the judge of humanity (John 5:22). He accepted prayers and worship—which mere mortals and angels rejected (Acts 10:25-26; Revelation 22:8-9). He was conceived by the Holy Spirit. Furthermore, divine attributes are attributed to Him such as being eternal (John 1:1), omnipresent (present everywhere, Matthew 18:20), and omniscient (all-knowing, Luke 6:8; John 2:24-25). He was also considered omnipotent (all-powerful), having performed more than thirty-five miracles recorded in the Gospels. He was immutable (never changing, Hebrews 13:8). The biblical case for Jesus' deity is also indisputable.

The mystery lies in understanding how the two natures relate to one another in the single person of Jesus. How do we reconcile such radically different natures in one being? During the first five centuries of church history, the church fathers debated possible explanations and rejected six positions—later catalogued as heretical—prior to reaching an understanding that fully honors the revealed text of Scripture.

COMMON MISCONCEPTIONS OF JESUS' DUAL NATURE

Any attempt to understand Jesus' dual nature must consider what is clearly revealed in the Bible—Jesus was fully human and fully divine. Numerous attempts to unlock the mystery of Jesus' dual nature ended up misrepresenting one of Jesus' natures or misunderstanding how they related to one another. Let's briefly consider the six rejected views.

1. **Ebionism**. This view negated Jesus' divine nature by denying His pre-existence. They believed Jesus became divine *after* His water baptism when the Holy Spirit descended upon him.
2. **Docetism**. This view negated Jesus' human nature by arguing that Jesus only appeared to be human, when in reality, He was only divine.
3. **Arianism**. This view denied Jesus' *full* deity. They believed Jesus was divine, but inferior to God the Father.
4. **Nestorianism**. This view argued that there were two persons. In this view, the divine person exerted control over the human.
5. **Eutychianism**. This view denied the distinctions between the two natures of Jesus. They argued that the divine nature somehow swallowed up the human nature, and a third nature arose.
6. **Apollinarianism**. This view denied Jesus' full humanity. They argued that Jesus did not have a human spirit. In other words, Jesus had two natures, but only one spirit.

These perspectives were dismissed as heretical because they did not account for the clear biblical emphasis on Jesus' human and divine natures. The importance of preserving both natures is highlighted by Erickson, "If the redemption accomplished on the cross is to avail for humankind, it must be the work of the human Jesus. But if it is to have the infinite value necessary to atone for the sins of all human beings in relationship to an infinite and perfectly holy God, then it must be the work of the divine Christ as well. If the death of the Savior is not the work of a unified God-man, it will be deficient at one point or the other."[96]

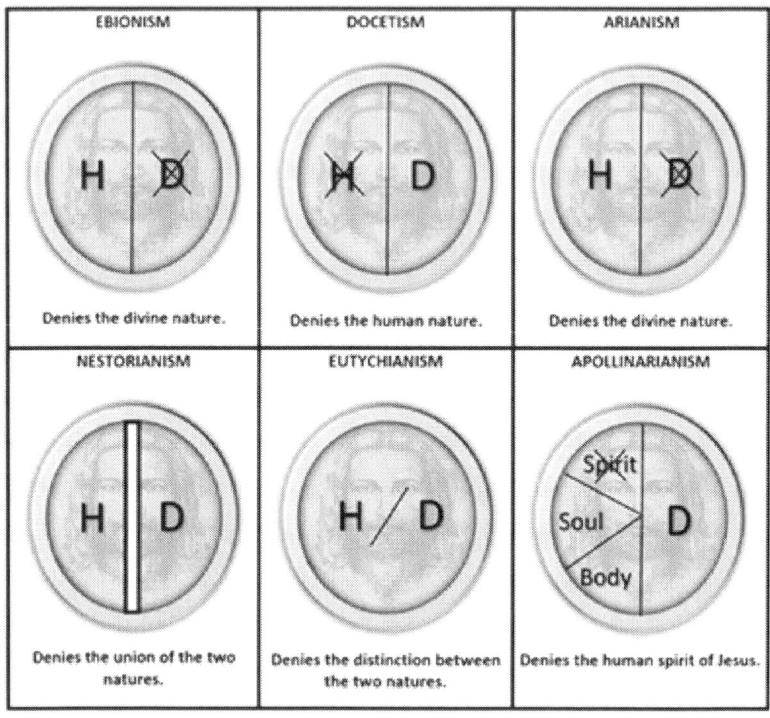

Six Christological Heresies[97]

That is why the church fathers—at the Council of Chalcedon (451 AD)—acknowledged the position that has been the foundation of Christology for thirteen centuries. Among the precise declarations that we find in the creed, it is confirmed that in order to understand the dual nature of Jesus, it is necessary to affirm that He is, "truly God and truly man, of a reasonable soul and body; consubstantial with the Father according to the Godhead and consubstantial with us according to the manhood; ...Christ, Son,

[96]Millard Erickson, *Christian Theology*, 2nd Edition (Grand Rapids: Baker Books, 1998), 740.

[97]Adapted with modifications from H. Wayne House, *Charts of Christian Theology & Doctrine* (Grand Rapids: Zondervan Publishing House, 1992), 55.

Lord, Only-begotten, to be acknowledged in two natures, inconfusedly, unchangeably, indivisibly, inseparably."[98] Thus, any response with regards to Jesus' limitations must take His dual nature into account. Failure to do so constitutes a misrepresentation of Jesus as He is revealed in Scripture. So, how does this knowledge apply to the question at hand?

DEALING WITH JESUS' LIMITATIONS

Every question we ask regarding Jesus has two possible responses—one according to His human nature and one according to His divine nature. For example, did Jesus experience physical exhaustion? The answer is yes and no. In His human nature He did get tired, but in His divine nature He did not. Did Jesus experience hunger and thirst? In His human nature He did experience hunger and thirst; nevertheless, as God, He did not. Quite the contrary, He is the Bread of Life and the Fountain of Living Water.

In His human nature Jesus experienced physical growth, had to learn to walk and to talk, and developed as any human being. But as God, Jesus is eternal, omniscient, and immutable (He doesn't grow, learn, or change). So, when we ask if there were things Jesus did not know, the answer would also be yes and no. As God, He is omniscient (all-knowing), but as a human, there were things He did not know. That is exactly what we observe in the Gospels. There were things Jesus did not know, including the date of the second coming. On the other hand, Jesus knew things that no human could possibly know. For example, He revealed to the Samaritan woman all that she had done. On other occasions, the Gospels tell us that Jesus knew what the scribes and Pharisees were thinking. Both of His natures are clearly seen.

CONCLUSION

How did Jesus manage both natures? We have no idea whatsoever. Here we have a legitimate mystery. But a mystery is not a contradiction. The apparent paradox regarding Jesus' limited knowledge results from not taking His dual nature into account. When He responded to the disciples that He did not know the date of the second coming, He was not being deceitful. In His human nature, He really did not know. However, this lack of knowledge in no way diminishes His divine nature. As God, He knows all things.

---

[98]G. A. Jackson, *The Post-Nicene Fathers* (New York: D. Appleton and Company, 1883), 24

Chapter 28

WHY DOES A "GOOD" GOD ALLOW BAD THINGS TO HAPPEN?

JUAN VALDES

One-thousand-one, one-thousand-two, one-thousand-three–that's how long it took for a twelve-story beachfront condominium in Surfside, Florida, to collapse into a mountain of rubble—taking the lives of ninety-eight men, women, and children. A security video from a building across the street captured the horrible three seconds it took for the entire structure to collapse at approximately 1:25 a.m. on June 24, 2021. Couldn't God have kept that building from falling? Why would God allow such a horrible tragedy? Every story of every victim is overwhelmingly tragic. Sadly, this story is just a drop in the bucket compared to the enormous amount of pain, suffering, and evil experienced daily on planet Earth. What are we to make of it all? How do we reconcile the existence of a benevolent, all-mighty God, and the existence of so much suffering, pain, and evil in the world He created? These are tough questions.

To tackle this problem, it is vital to understand that this is not just a difficult issue for Christianity: Every religion or worldview must grapple with it as well. In this response, we will take a brief look at how different worldviews attempt to answer the question of why we experience pain and suffering and discover that they fall far short of providing satisfying answers. Then we will consider the problem from the perspective of a Christian worldview. In doing so, we will tackle five tough but relevant questions and see that the Christian worldview offers the most comprehensive and satisfactory answers to the problem of evil and suffering. Finally, we will consider some of the reasons God allows suffering and pain in our world.

IT'S NOT JUST OUR PROBLEM

Imagine this headline: "Drowning in doubt, Asia rebukes God."[99] That was the headline in the Spanish version of the Sunday edition of the *Miami Herald* on January 2, 2005. A devastating tsunami hit Indonesia a week prior, on December 26, 2004, killing over 227,000 people across a dozen countries. It was probably the most devastating natural disaster recorded in modern history. The aforementioned newspaper article was unique in that it afforded us a view into how different worldviews see the problem of pain and suffering. Reporters interviewed people from different religions and worldviews to get a feel for how they dealt with this tragedy. Their responses were very telling.

Hinduism's response is as varied as the religion itself. An old lady from Tamil Nadu in South India said, "*God, why have you done this? What did we do to upset you?*" From her perspective, God is some sort of deity that lashes out in anger and slaughters innocent people that have done nothing to provoke Him. Ananth Subramania-Batter, a Hindu high priest, said that "*the souls of those who died in South Asia live on, and they will reincarnate, maybe in human form, maybe as animals or insects. It depends on the karma of the person, determined by the way they lived in this life.*" This response makes it obvious that the Hindu response to the problem of pain and suffering is detestable. If you think a lifetime (70-80 years) of suffering and pain is hard, imagine

[99]The title and all quotes regarding this article are my translation from the original text in Spanish. The original article is written by Peter Graff / Reuters- London and appeared in El Herald en Español, Sunday Jan. 2, 2005. The article was titled, *"Ahogada en dudas, Asia increpa a Dios,"* 19a.

a worldview where you die, come back, and endure another lifetime of pain and suffering–and then do it again, and again, and again, etc. Hinduism offers no hope of ever finding a solution to the problem of pain and suffering, because to escape the cycle of reincarnation would require living a perfect life, which nobody can do.

Islam's response to the problem is quite problematic as well. Hasem Bazian, Professor of Islam at UC Berkeley at the time of the article, quoted the hadith and said that "*in Islam, all those who die in a catastrophe, die as martyrs; their sins are not taken into account, and they are allowed into paradise*." This response may seem comforting to those who lost a loved one in the disaster, but what about justice?

Are they saying rapists, child molesters, serial killers, and the like will enter paradise so long as they are in the right place at the right time and die in a catastrophe? Really?? Azizan Abdul Razak, a Muslim cleric, said the disaster was a message from God reminding man that "*He created the world, and He can destroy it!*" This seems to speak of a God that needs to be continuously proving Himself to man and is willing to allow such events to prove He has the authority to do such things.

According to New Age "theology" and the *Gaia Hypothesis*, the tsunami was the result of the rage of Earth, which is a living organism. Until man finds peace and harmony and stops attempting to destroy her, she will continue to punish man through her extraordinary power. However, this idea that our planet is a conscious being determined to "teach us a lesson" is the kind that makes for great science fiction.

Another worldview that cannot make heads or tails of the problem of suffering and pain is Deism. According to some deists, God couldn't avoid the tsunami, He could only respond to the tragedy after the fact. Another deist argued that God is not sovereign, nor is He really in control of the universe—He only controls parts of it and He isn't really perfect either. So, he suggests that we learn to think of God in different terms: "*But if we can bring ourselves to acknowledge that there are some things God does not control, many good things become possible*."[100]

---

[100]Harold S. Kushner. *When Bad Things Happen to Good People* (New York: Anchor Books, 1981), 45.

However, if this is correct, then why do we call God, "God"? This deist adds,"*Are you capable of forgiving God even when you have found out that He is not perfect…?*"[101] He twists the question with the claim that now *we* are the ones doing the forgiving.

Even this brief consideration of how people outside the *Christian* worldview see the problem of suffering, pain, and evil highlights the ineffectiveness of their approaches, so let's examine how the Christian worldview deals with this problem.

TACKLING THE HARD QUESTIONS

Because the problem of pain and suffering is so complex and involves so many factors, I will approach it by considering five tough questions that stem from our human attempts to wrap our minds around the problem. Each of these questions presents a direct challenge to the Christian worldview, but each can be answered in ways that are intellectually satisfying.

1. **Why didn't God make a world where people did not hurt each other?**

   Actually, He did! When Adam and Eve were created, they had no desire or inclination towards causing each other pain or suffering. The world God created was good—a fact attested to by the phrase "*…and God saw that it was good.*" This phrase appears five times in Genesis chapter one with regards to the environment in which God placed Adam and Eve. Regarding the finished creative work of God, which included animals and humans, Genesis 1:31 tells us, "God saw all that he had made, and it was very good."

2. **Did God create evil? If not, then where did evil come from?**

   If the world God created was so good, how did evil enter this world? Is evil one of the "good" things God created?

---

[101]Ibid., 148.

Absolutely NOT! God is not the creator of evil. Quite the contrary, the Bible teaches that every good and every perfect gift comes from God (James 1:17). So, where did evil come from? How could evil come from a "perfect" creation?

Let's begin by defining the word "*evil.*" The key to understanding the *origin* of evil lies in understanding the *nature* of evil. Apologists Norman Geisler & R.M. Brooks break it down in easy-to-understand terms by explaining that evil is not some substance that grabs hold of certain things and makes them bad, like a virus. Evil is not a rival force in the universe, like the dark side of Luke Skywalker's force. As a matter of fact, evil is not something at all—it's not a substance. Evil is a *lack of* or *corruption of* things. When the good *that should be there* is missing or corrupted, that is evil. If a man lacks the ability to see (which should be there), that is evil. If a person lacks the kindness in his heart and respect for human life (that should be there), then he may commit murder or other evil acts. Evil, in reality, is a parasite that cannot exist except as a hole in something that should be solid.[102]

But how does this apply to the perfect creation of God? How could a perfect Adam and Eve do something wrong, like disobey God? Again, following Geisler & Brooks' argument, one of the things that makes men morally perfect is our freedom to make real choices about what we do. God made us perfect beings, and that perfection included freedom. To be free, we had to have not only the opportunity to choose good, but also the ability *not* to choose good. That was a risk God knowingly took. That doesn't make Him responsible for evil: He created the *fact* of freedom; we perform the *acts* of freedom. Evil was *possible* because of free choice, but man made

---

[102]Adapted from Norman Geisler & R. M. Brooks. *When Skeptics Ask* (Wheaton, IL: Victor Books, 1990), 61.

evil *actual*. Imperfection came through the abuse of our moral perfection as free creatures.[103]

3. **Why didn't God make us unable to choose to do things that cause pain, and suffering?**

Why did God take that risk? Why give us such freedom? We were created to love God and love one another. But to choose to love God, man must be able to choose not to as well. After all, if we don't have a choice, it isn't love. If you hold a gun to someone's head and ask them if they love you, their response is meaningless. If you purchase the latest doll and press the button where she says, "I love you" repeatedly, those words are meaningless. Likewise, to choose to obey God, man must be able to choose not to obey Him. Otherwise, we are not really free beings. Adam and Eve used their perfect freedom to choose to disobey God—and in doing so, they introduced evil into God's perfect creation.[104]

4. **Couldn't God have anticipated the consequences of giving people free choice?**

He did! In God's omniscience, He knew the exact course that human history would take. He knew this before He created the universe. He knew Adam and Eve would fall; He knew how wicked the hearts of man would become. He knew He would have to hit the reset button and destroy an entire civilization with a global flood. He knew that many would violate His first covenant. He knew that the Son would have to come and die a horrible

---

[103]Ibid., 62.

[104]Satan, no doubt, had a role in Adam and Eve's decision. He attempted to persuade them to use their freedom to make a bad choice—and he succeeded. However, he is not to blame for evil entering this world, because Adam and Eve made the choice—they were not forced to do so. Interestingly, that is the same choice Satan himself made in the angelic realm. He too, as a perfect being, used his freedom to choose to rebel against his Creator and persuaded other angels to do the same. He introduced evil in the angelic realm.

death on the cross to save mankind. He knew about all the struggles, wars, famines, diseases, etc. that would corrupt His perfect creation on account of sin. BUT, He also knew the millions and millions of people that would freely choose to love Him and spend an eternity with Him in Heaven—and so He said, “Let us make man.” He saw the “big picture” and determined that the result outweighed the process required to get there.

5. Why can’t evil be stopped?

If God is benevolent and all powerful, why does it seem as if He cannot stop the spread of evil? Given that God knows all things from the beginning, it isn’t hard to see that if evil is a part of human history, then it definitely plays a role in achieving the end results for which God created the universe. We must understand that evil cannot be destroyed without destroying the very freedom that makes us able to choose to love. Thus, if freedom were destroyed, which seems to be the only way to end evil, that would be evil in itself. It would deprive free creatures of their greatest good. If evil is to be dealt with, we need to talk about *overcoming* evil, rather than *destroying* it. Note also that just because evil has not yet been dealt with does not mean it will never be dealt with. The Bible makes it clear that God is all-good and all-powerful and that He will one day permanently defeat evil. Evil *will* be stopped!

Given that God knows all things from the beginning, it isn’t hard to see that if evil is a part of human history, then it definitely plays a role in achieving the end results for which God created the universe.

While there are many other questions that could be raised around this topic, these seem to be the most important in understanding how evil has entered God's perfect creation and why it has not yet been stopped. Now, let's shift our focus from the philosophical discussion above to a more practical consideration of the topic. Why does God allow evil, pain, and suffering to afflict us in our everyday lives?

IS THERE A PURPOSE FOR THE SUFFERING AND PAIN?

There is an amazing passage in the Bible that provides a type of "umbrella" under which we can consider the various ways in which pain and suffering may actually be useful in our everyday lives. The Apostle Paul, in one of his most powerful passages, tells us that "we know that for those who love God all things work together for good, for those who are called according to His purpose" (Romans 8:28). But what does that look like in everyday life? To answer that, we need to understand our limitations.

Unlike God, we don't see the big picture. We often find that suffering and pain doesn't seem to make any sense to us. However, our individual lives can be compared to pieces in a giant jigsaw puzzle that consists of billions of pieces. From our limited perspective, it is impossible for us to see how all of the pieces fit together. This is where faith comes in. We need to trust that the "puzzle maker" has designed each piece to fit together to achieve the final product He desires. Nevertheless, the Bible does provide insight into some of the reasons why God allows pain and suffering in our lives.[105]

- First, pain and suffering provide a way for us to grow in character and spiritual strength. In other words, pain and suffering often serve as training opportunities in our lives. Paul explained this to us when he wrote, "we rejoice in our sufferings, knowing that suffering produces endurance, and endurance produces character, and character produces hope" (Romans 5:3-4). It's hard to imagine developing endurance without having to suffer through trials and tribulations.

[105]This list of four purposes is by no means meant to be exhaustive. There seem to be other reasons provided in the Bible, but these should suffice for the purposes of this response.

- Second, pain and suffering are often used as incentives to consider a midcourse correction. When we stray from the path, God may allow us to experience the consequences of our poor choices so that we will stop and return to the path He has set out for us.

- Third, we find that God uses negative situations to bring forth a greater good. Think of the life of Joseph as an example. All his apparently random suffering turned out to be a purposeful path that placed him as Egypt's second in command—a position from which he was able to save the lives of his entire family, as well as thousands of others. While we usually don't get to see the purpose of the suffering and pain in our lifetime, Joseph saw it and uttered this confident declaration in Genesis 50:20: "You meant evil against me, but God meant it for good." Yet another example of a positive from a negative is the cross of Christ. All the pain and suffering Christ endured on the cross turned out to be good news for the salvation of mankind.

From our limited perspective, it is impossible for us to see how all of the pieces fit together. This is where faith comes in.

- Finally, God often allows pain and suffering in our lives to get our attention. C.S. Lewis put it best, "God whispers to us in our pleasures, speaks in our conscience, but shouts in our pains; it is His megaphone to rouse a deaf world."[106]

CONCLUSION

Suffering, pain, and evil are a reality that all worldviews must attempt to understand. A brief look at how some of the major worldviews

---

[106] C.S. Lewis. *The Problem of Pain* (San Francisco: Harper Collins, 1996), 91.

tackle the problem makes it rather obvious that there are no easy answers—these worldviews fail to provide an intellectually satisfying answer. On the other hand, the Christian worldview provides the most exhaustive treatise of the problem—one which many find far superior to the alternatives. When the hard questions are approached from a Christian worldview, the answers are rational and cohere perfectly with what we know about the world we live in. In addition, the Christian worldview provides much insight into the possible purposes for why God may allow pain and suffering in our lives. From God's perspective, Revelation chapters 21 and 22 provide a preview of the "big picture," showing us that evil will, in the end, be dealt with definitively. We must trust that God knows what He is doing.

EPILOGUE

Well, I hope after reading this you've been encouraged! I still remember as a child being told to NOT ask questions in church. It went something like: "Good boys don't ask those questions," or "Children are to be seen, and not heard," or simply being pawned off on somebody else when I did ask a question.

Body of Christ, we can't do that anymore. Parents, please become a hero to your child by taking what they're struggling with and working through it with them. I understand that you don't have all the answers to their questions; the truth is, none of us do. But when we don't know the answer to a question, we can set a pattern for our children to follow: Take them with you as you search for answers! Hopefully, this book will be something you can read with your children–and, consequently, you will find yourself having meaningful conversations with them!

I don't think there's anything, other than sharing the Gospel with our children, that we can do to better prepare them for the craziness that we see in the world around us. I literally just got back from a camp (summer 2021) where one of the students asked the following question:

> *For everyone that knows me, there's a different version of me that lives in their head. For example, who I think I am is different than who I actually am. Same goes for everyone who knows me and who they think I am is the version of me that lives in their head.*
>
> *The same goes for the Bible. It's impossible to preach the Bible the same way, it's impossible for your version of me to be perfect. You can only preach your version of the Bible. If you think something false is true, it's just as true to you as something that's actually true. I actually think it's possible to grossly mis-interpret the Bible, and I think it's impossible to know how*

> *accurate your interpretation of the Bible is. The odds of your interpretation being 100% accurate are next to impossible.*
>
> *So, my question is, how can you feel confident in your interpretation of the Bible and be comfortable preaching that interpretation knowing that you're probably spreading lies? At least to a certain degree.*

I know that's more commentary than question, but we give the students the freedom to express themselves. I thought I'd share my response with you.

> "From your statements, you make it clear that we can make something that is NOT true, true, just by believing that it's true. Also, that writings can have multiple meanings depending on how the reader interprets them–that I can read something and have a totally different interpretation than what the author intended. So, with that being the standard that you've set, here's my response. Thank you for an excellent recipe for apple pie, I just think it doesn't have enough sugar added. Other than that, though, it looks really good!"

After giving this response, a young man (whom I later found out wrote this initial question) sat looking at me with daggers in his eyes. He didn't say a word, but the following is what I expected to have taken place:

> ***Youth***: What? I didn't write anything about a pie recipe!
>
> ***Carl***: Yes, yes you did, when I read this, I see a pie recipe, but it needs more sugar!
>
> ***Youth***: It doesn't say that.
>
> ***Carl***: Oh, but you told me that I can read something and understand it differently than what the author meant. So, that's what I believe you meant. Also, since I believe it, I'm not lying! As

> a matter of fact, there's no such thing as a lie under your belief system, because if I believe what I'm saying is true, then it is true. So, why would you accuse me of lying?

The young man didn't change his opinion. Hopefully, he has food for thought for the future. We don't convict or convert; the Holy Spirit does. We converse and give answers for why we have hope and watch what the Lord will do with our obedience.

One last story from this same camp: On day one, I received the following statement on one of the index cards: "*I believe in god, but I don't believe he made Earth or people. I believe we evolved from apes and Earth was created by multiple mediors (sic) combined. I believe in science but when you need god and he's the only one that could help. I believe in praying.*"

My response was:

> At the risk of sounding like a jerk there's no question here, just statements. So, I'll just address the statements. First, you don't understand science. And that's because science doesn't teach that apes evolved into humans. When we make that claim, we tell those who do understand the current version of evolution that we don't understand it. The current theory teaches that an 'ape-like' ancestor evolved into apes and humans. This ape-like ancestor had both human and ape features and over the years as they procreated, some of the offspring acquired more of the human features and some of the offspring gradually acquired the ape features, and after millions of years, we have apes and humans. One did NOT come from the other. And science doesn't teach that meteors crashed together to become the Earth. But, even if it did, where did these meteors come from? Hydrogen gas came from nothing so that it could explode to become something that eventually became everything?? I don't think so.
>
> Second, you don't understand the God of the Bible. To think that He's just someone that you pray to when you need help makes Him nothing more than a genie in a bottle that you rub to get a wish when needed. He's like a lucky rabbit's foot that you hook

> onto your belt loop just in case. That's NOT the God who revealed Himself in Scripture. The biblical God is the one who created all things, including you and me. The One Who loved us so much that while we were spitting on Him, He willingly went to a cross and died for us. If you want value, there it is. NOTHING can give you more value than the fact that the One who created all things loves us and made us in His image. I'd encourage you to do some more studying on these topics and hopefully the rest of this week will help answer some questions and encourage you to dig deeper.

I didn't know who that student was. I just tried to be honest and straightforward without ridiculing. During this camp week, I spoke fourteen times. At most of the camps that I've been to, the speakers typically just focus on messages that deal with the heart–and those are important, please don't misunderstand me. BUT God says we're to love Him with all our "heart, soul, **mind,** and strength" (emphasis added). So, of the fourteen talks I gave, thirteen of them dealt with the questions these youth had asked that focused on the mind!

NOTHING can give you more value than the fact that the One who created all things loves us and made us in His image.

By the way, many of those questions are in this book. On the last night, my talk was directed at the heart. After the talk, I gave an altar call, and ten young men and women responded. What a blessed moment! Two young men were sobbing so hard they couldn't speak. One of those young men came up and gave me a huge hug. Through sobs, he explained to me that he was the one that had written that statement on day one. He said he had never heard that Christianity had anything to offer to the craziness that he sees in his everyday world.

The young man's counselor came up to me afterwards and was nearly in tears. He told me, "I can't believe what just happened. The two young men that came up sobbing were in my cabin all week. They were the worst of the worst. I didn't think there was any chance they would change!"

God is still in the life-changing business! All of us who contributed to this book PRAY that these answers don't come across as if we're trying to impress anyone with our knowledge and make people feel stupid. That's NOT the goal. We're fellow pilgrims on the journey of life. We simply desire to see folks excited about their faith and standing firm on the rock-solid foundation of the Word of God. May God richly bless and keep you. May you shine in the darkness and love people enough to give an answer for the reason of the hope that's within you, with meekness and fear! Most importantly—**Stay Bold**!

Isa. 41:10-13

Carl Kerby

ABOUT THE AUTHORS/EDITORS

CARL KERBY, CONTRIBUTING WRITER AND EDITOR

As President and Co-Founder of Reasons for Hope* Inc., Carl's passion is to train and equip the next generation to be able to stand boldly on the Word of God. He received Jesus Christ as his Lord and Savior on May 15, 1987; two years later, he was introduced to the importance of biblical authority at a Back to Genesis Conference. This experience made such an impact on him that for the next six years, he volunteered at these conferences across the globe. In 1993, Carl was invited to serve on the Board of Directors for Answers in Genesis (AiG). Ten years later, he joined AiG as a full-time speaker and Vice President for Ministry Relations. Starting in 2010, the Lord burdened Carl to focus solely on reaching the younger generation. To accomplish this calling, he left AiG and co-created Reasons for Hope* Inc. (RforH) in January 2011.

Carl has been married to his wife, Masami, for over 40 years. They live in Northern Kentucky and enjoy time spent with their two children, five grandchildren, and a beagle pup named Snoopy Deux.

JUAN VALDES, CONTRIBUTING WRITER AND EDITOR

Juan is the Senior Pastor of a Spanish-speaking congregation and a senior speaker and writer with RforH. He has a passion for youth and apologetics and has worked with young people for many years as a Christian middle and high school Chaplain and teacher of Bible and Introduction to Philosophy. His love for learning and teaching led to graduate work at Trinity Evangelical Divinity School, as well as master's degrees from both Liberty Baptist Theological Seminary and Logos Graduate School. He also holds a Doctor of Ministry degree in Apologetics from Southern Evangelical Seminary. Juan has taught

Theology, Bible, and Apologetics at the seminary level in *both* English and Spanish and is an influential promoter of apologetics in the greater Miami area. He speaks regularly across the country and internationally at pastor's conferences, youth conferences, summer camps, apologetics conferences, and local church events.

Juan and his wife Daisy have been married for 34 years and have two college-age kids, Juan Elias and Jessica. Together they serve in multiple areas of ministry in Miami, Florida.

Frank Figueroa, Contributing Writer

Frank is currently pastoring a church in Hawaii and has been thrilled to serve alongside Carl Kerby and the rest of the RforH team as a speaker. As a teenager, Frank had an ambition to be a rock star, but a friend invited him to a Bible study in the fall of 1985, and there he found himself being confronted by the authority of God's Word. Within five minutes, Frank's life was never the same. His education includes a degree in science education, as well as studies in theology and music. He and his wife, April, love serving together and, out of their interest in bow-hunting, formed Centershot Hawaii, an archery ministry to reach out to the children in their community. This outreach has taken them as far as American Samoa and Romania! It is through God's grace and mercy that Frank can share the good news of God's Son, Jesus, with as many people as He will allow...To Him be all honor, glory, and praise, now and forever more.

Dave Glander, Contributing Writer

Dave joined RforH in 2021 where he serves as a speaker and writer, as well as the leader of our Mic'd Up ministry. His story began in a strongly non-Christian environment where he naturally became a devout atheist. When he was thirty years old, he was on the brink of suicide and desperately cried out to a God whom he didn't even believe existed. It was at this moment that Dave was dramatically changed and filled with inexplicable peace. He had no choice but to accept the fact that a supernatural God must exist after all. He began to study various world religions, found them lacking, and was given the book, "A Case for Christ," which included the information he was seeking. Not only did he acknowledge Jesus as the One true God and his personal Savior, but he was also introduced to the discipline of apologetics. He is now a deeply committed believer in Jesus Christ and the Bible.

Dave also founded EQUIP Retreat, an apologetics summer camp training students with absolute truth to support their Christian faith, empowering them to own their faith, and challenging them to develop the boldness to share it with others. He has taught at national and regional conferences, universities, churches, and youth camps around the country. Dave currently lives in the Atlanta area with his wife, Stephanie, and is the proud parent of Marc, who is married to Alyssa.

D. Marc Jacobs, Jr., Contributing Writer

As Senior Vice President of Operations at Penneco Oil Company and its affiliates, Marc oversees all functional areas associated with oil and gas exploration and production; however, his original degree is in theology. The nexus of these experiences and passion for both has given him a unique perspective that has opened doors of opportunity in the field of education. For many years, he taught evening classes at Western Pennsylvania Theological Institute as well as modular courses at other institutes of learning. Marc's lectures are primarily focused on *Origins and the History of the Ancients* using a biblical worldview.

Marc and his wife, Sheila, have been married for 37 years and have two daughters with young families of their own–one lives near them in Pennsylvania, and the other daughter lives in Ireland. They are known by their three grandchildren as Lolli and Pops.

Bub Kuns, Contributing Writer

Bub is the Creative Director for RforH and the producer of our DeBunked videos, DeBunked TV series, and the Bub and Bob Show. In his early years, he scared his parents by writing short horror stories in red ink. They learned to embrace it and prayed it would turn into something more constructive one day. Years later, through a series of films, teachers and church leaders, Bub placed his full trust in the redemptive work of Jesus. Since then, he has had a passion to reach people for Christ in creative and entertaining ways. He has served in other venues as Creative Director, Chief Content Director, Elder, and Associate Pastor, and is the founder and president of a video agency in southern California that works on video content for Fortune 100 brands and non-profits like PragerU. Bub lives in Texas with his wife and daughter.

Dan Lietha, Contributing Writer and Illustrator

Dan joined RforH in 2019 as our cartoonist and illustrator, developing images and speaker slides that challenge viewers to think biblically. "Truth Jabs" is his newest cartoon feature, and he also produces an online educational video series called "Draw It & Know It!" instructing viewers on how to draw animals and think about them with a biblical worldview. Dan was impacted at a very young age by two things that dramatically directed the course of his life … receiving Jesus Christ as his Lord and Savior and drawing! After high school, he attended and graduated from the Joe Kubert School of Cartoon and Graphic Art in 1987. Three years later, a biblical creation video series titled "Understanding Genesis" began a growing hunger in Dan to learn about biblical creation and the foundations of the Christian faith. One message in that video series inspired Dan to develop a comic strip called CreationWise. Eventually, that comic strip led Dan to volunteer (and later work for) the ministry that became Answers in Genesis as full-time cartoonist and illustrator.

Dan loves camp ministry and has spoken at camps and other venues over the past 15 years. He lives in northern Kentucky with his wife, Marcia, and daughter, Hannah.

Candace Nordine, Contributing Writer

Candace is the Communications Manager and "Knower of All Stuff" at RforH. She grew up as a PK (pastor's kid), and though she had a knowledge of who God was from a very young age, it wasn't until her middle school years that she truly made her faith her own. Serving in full-time ministry for the past two decades, Candace understands the need for the next generation to have biblical answers that will help equip them to stand boldly on the Word of God.

Candace is a wife, mom, teacher, employee, cook, interior decorator, designer, etc., but her greatest role is being a daughter of the King. She is thankful that God uses ordinary people just like her (1 Corinthians 1:26-31). She currently lives in northern Kentucky with her amazing husband and four very cool daughters who keep her young and hip.

David Ross, Contributing Writer

David Ross began his career as a psychologist after obtaining his Doctor of Psychology in Clinical Psychology, but in December 2005, a whole new life began after encountering Jesus Christ. Subsequently, he obtained a Master of Divinity in Christian Apologetics from Veritas Evangelical Seminary. David continues to joyfully use the education, experience, and skills that God has given him to serve his community and his local church. Having worked with countless people in clinical practice, as well as in his ministerial capacity, David has invested his life in helping others to make choices that will honor God and others. His book, *Choosing for Two: An Examination of Abortion Decision Making and Its Implications for Crisis Counseling*, resulted from his desire to combine the experience and skills God has provided with his passion for saving the unborn.

David is a bi-vocational pastor and healthcare administrator who currently resides in the Pacific Northwest with his wife and daughter.

Brian Scoggin, Contributing Writer

Brian serves as a part-time speaker with RforH. He served for twelve years as drummer for the Christian musical group Casting Crowns, which provided him with the privileged opportunity to witness God at work across the United States and much of the world. Brian now leads a young church that meets in his home in collaboration with The Gathering Place Network, as well as serving as regional director with Families 4 Families, a Christian foster care agency that works to place vulnerable children in Christian homes. In addition to these two ministries, Brian loves to share his passion for God as he travels and speaks with RforH.

He lives in Griffin, Georgia, with his wife, Ivy, and their two sons, Brady and Max. Brian and his family are committed to making

God known through the teaching of His Word and their way of life. He believes that true joy is found when God is glorified above all things in a person's life.

Hannah Dukes, Editor, Proofreader, and Contributing Writer

Hannah currently volunteers as an editor, proofreader, and writer for RforH. She has always been fascinated with words, so the opportunity to preview and edit this book has been a combination of this love of words with her love of the truth of Jesus Christ and the way His truth affects every part of our lives. It has been an honor to come alongside the authors of these articles and be blessed, impacted, and challenged by what they share. Her prayer is that God would use this book in mighty ways to impact the next generation! She is very happily married to her husband, Shannon, and homeschools their two children.

Holly Varnum, Editor and Proofreader

Holly joined RforH in 2021 and currently serves as our Director of Curriculum Development. With degrees in education, curriculum and instruction, and educational administration, Holly has decades of experience in working with teens and adults in camp ministry, teaching and administration, and curriculum writing (A Beka Book, Focus on the Family, and Answers in Genesis to name a few). Saved at a very young age and serving the Lord ever since, she has a passion for God's truth and communicating it with others. She is so thankful God has provided her with a well-rounded perspective through service as a classroom teacher, instructional coach, administrator, camp counselor, Sunday School teacher, ladies' Bible Study teacher, and conference speaker.

Along with her husband, Paul, (Director of Media Content for RforH), she enjoys any time they can spend with their three grown daughters, two sons-in-law, and two grandchildren (so far!). She lives in the beautiful state of Maine, and yes, eats lobster (properly pronounced "lobstah") whenever she gets a chance!

Want even *more* answers?

Find our other books and more resources at:

rforh.com

reasons*for*hope*

Made in United States
Troutdale, OR
10/23/2023

13939645R00133